audiobooks for youth

audiobooks for youth

A Practical Guide to Sound Literature

Mary Burkey

ala editions

An imprint of the American Library Association
CHICAGO   2013

MARY BURKEY is a National Board–certified teacher-librarian from Columbus, Ohio. She is the past chair of the American Library Association's Notable Children's Recordings, was part of the Odyssey Award Task Force, and served as the chair of ALA's first Odyssey Award for Excellence in Audiobook Production Committee. She currently serves as a judge for the Audio Publishers Association's Audie Awards, reviews for *Booklist* magazine and *The Horn Book* magazine, and writes *Booklist*'s audiobook column "Voices in My Head." Her Audiobooker blog (http://audiobooker .booklistonline.com) serves as an online scrapbook of audiobook minutiae, digital literature ramblings, and reflections on audio productions and performances.

Printed in the United States of America
17 16 15 14 13   5 4 3 2 1

Extensive effort has gone into ensuring the reliability of the information in this book; however, the publisher makes no warranty, express or implied, with respect to the material contained herein.

ISBNs: 978–0-8389-1157-0 (paper); 978-0-8389-9587-7 (PDF); 978-0-8389-9588-4 (ePub); 978-0-8389-9589-1 (Kindle). For more information on digital formats, visit the ALA Store at alastore.ala.org and select eEditions.

Library of Congress Cataloging-in-Publication Data

Burkey, Mary.
    Audiobooks for youth : a practical guide to sound literature /
    Mary Burkey.
        pages   cm
    Includes bibliographical references and index.
    ISBN 978-0-8389-1157-0 (alk. paper)
    1. Libraries—Special collections—Children's audiobooks. 2. Children's audiobooks—United States. I. Title.
    Z688.A93B87 2013
    025.2'882—dc23   2012022639

Cover design by Kirstin Krutsch. Cover images © Shutterstock, Inc.
Text design by Kimberly Thornton in Miso Light and Charis SIL.

♾ This paper meets the requirements of ANSI/NISO Z39.48–1992 (Permanence of Paper).

Dedicated to the members of the audiobook community
who so willingly shared their expertise and personal
reflections, with gratitude and appreciation

CONTENTS

1 A History of Children's Audiobooks

ONCE UPON A TIME, there was the word. The word was shaped into the sound of story and flowed through time and place, carried by the teller's voice. In daily life, spoken word served as the foundation of culture. Mother soothed her child with story; heroes were immortalized in legend; elders passed along their knowledge of the land through myth and tale. As sound took shape on the page, teachers and students recited lessons together, while religious leaders chanted holy words. The very act of reading was a social activity until the end of the Middle Ages, as the literate processed the meaning of text aloud until Western society instituted the practice of "private reading."[1] Well into the twentieth century, reading remained an aural activity as the newest serialized Sherlock Holmes tale was read aloud in the family parlor and Mark Twain traveled the country reciting his books on stage. Much of the language of literature recognizes this oral tradition; we speak of an author's *voice*, a work's *intended audience*, the writer's *tone, narrative sequence,* and *rhetorical mode.* The sound of story serves as a constant throughout history, conveyed by bard, safeguarded in script, captured by recording device, and transmitted by digital signal. Audiobooks connect us to literature in its original form, returning the listener to the virtual storyteller's circle.

Thomas Edison envisioned the power of aural literature to educate as well as amuse when he described the practical uses for recorded sound in his 1878 *North American Review* article "The Phonograph and its Future":

> *Books.*—Books may be read by the charitably inclined professional reader, or by such readers especially employed for that purpose, and the record of such book used in the asylums of the blind, hospitals, sick-chamber, or even with great profit and amusement by the lady or gentleman whose eyes and hands may be otherwise employed; or, again, because of the greater enjoyment to be had from a book when read by an elocutionist, than when read by the average reader. The ordinary record sheet, repeating this book from fifty to a hundred times as it will, would command a price that would pay the original reader well for the slightly increased difficulty in reading it aloud in the phonograph.

> *Educational Purposes.*—As an elocutionary teacher, or as a primary teacher for children, it will certainly be invaluable. By it, difficult passages may be correctly rendered for the pupil but once, after which he has only to apply to his phonograph for instructions. The child may thus learn to spell, commit to memory a lesson set for it, etc.[2]

With a stretch of the imagination, Edison might be credited with recording the first children's audiobook more than a century ago when, as he explains in a sound clip available on Project Gutenberg, Sarah Josepha Hale's poem "Mary Had a Little Lamb" was selected as the first experimental recording on his original tin cylinder phonograph in 1877.[3]

TALKING BOOKS EVOLVE

The publishing trade saw the first true combination of book-plus-recording in 1917 when Harper Columbia released *The Bubble Book*, a volume for children. This production was the twenty-sixth recording recognized by the Library of Congress National Recording Registry, established, as stated in the National Recording Preservation Act of 2000, to "maintain and preserve sound recordings and collections of sound recordings that are culturally, historically, or aesthetically significant."[4] The National Recording Registry citation reads:

> The Bubble Books, published by Harper Columbia between 1917 and 1922, was the first series of books and records published together especially for children. Authors were Ralph Mayhew and Burges Johnson, while Rhoda Chase provided the beautiful, full-color line drawings. Each book contained three 5½-inch discs to accompany the three nursery rhymes printed in the books. The singer is not listed on the discs, but is thought to be Henry Burr. Millions of the books were sold to delighted children in the U.S. and abroad.[5]

The charming Bubble Book series featured illustrated rhyming text, ranging from Mother Goose to *A Child's Garden of Verses,* in child-sized books with color-illustrated pages, which were joined within the book to serve as disc sleeves for small records containing the sung and spoken text. A November 1919 advertisement in *The Atlantic Monthly* notes that Bubble Books were available for one dollar at "any bookstore, Columbia Grafonoia store, gift shop, toy shop, music store, or department store" while the 1919 Sears catalog priced the titles at 89 cents. A massive November 1920 promotional effort in book trade journals described Harper Columbia's consumer push of the Bubble Books as "the largest campaign ever devoted to books" and created a rage for the recordings, which were marketed, despite copyright wrangles, into the early 1930s. In an early example of multimedia marketing, the vastly popular productions were endorsed by celebrity child actors, heralded at Bubble Book story times in bookstores, and played on the radio. The Bubble Books form the foundation of children's readalong audiobooks, creating a model of text, image, and words plus music that continues into the twenty-first century.[6]

As the sales of the Bubble Books succumbed to the Great Depression, the United States government took action on Edison's recommendation to use recorded books for the blind. In 1931, the Pratt-Smoot Act established the National Library Service for the Blind and Physically Handicapped (NLS), which charged the Librarian of Congress to establish a system to distribute Braille books through "local or regional centers for the circulation of such books, under such conditions and regulations as he may prescribe." In 1933, the NLS and the American Foundation for the Blind developed the Talking Book, a "recording on a disc of the voice of a good reader, and its reproduction at will through the instrumentality of a reproducing machine or phonograph." For decades, the NLS served only blind adults but was amended to include blind children in 1952 and expanded in 1966 to include those who have physical limitations, including reading disabilities that prevent the reading of standard print.[7]

The end of the Depression heralded a resurgence of recordings for children, bolstered by new nonbreakable vinyl 78 rpm discs and the development of long-playing LP records in 1948. In that pretelevision age, families gathered around the phonograph listening to releases from major labels which featured top stars and full orchestral accompaniment. Early children's recordings popularized abridged and adapted favorites such as Jean de Brunhoff's *Babar Stories* (Decca 1936), Dr. Seuss's *The 500 Hats of Bartholomew Cubbins* (RCA Victor 1940), Robert McCloskey's *Lentil* (Young People's Records 1946), and actor Jimmy Stewart's storybook-and-album of a pre-Disney *Winnie-the-Pooh* (RCA Victor 1953). Some standout examples of fully produced recordings include *A Christmas Carol* with Basil Rathbone (Columbia 1942); Orson Welles's adaptation of Oscar Wilde's fairy tale *The Happy Prince*, narrated by Welles and Bing Crosby, with original music composed by Academy Award–winner Bernard Herrmann (Decca 1946); and Ludwig Bemelmans's *Madeline* accompanied by Franz Schubert's symphonic music (RCA Victor 1953). Many a baby boomer will fondly recall their bright yellow, 25-cent unbreakable Little Golden Records of *The Poky Little Puppy* (1948) or *The Little Engine That Could* (1954).[8] In 2009 The National Recording Registry selected the Decca recording of *The Churkendoose* (1947), a classic representative from this era of children's recordings, for preservation in the Library of Congress, describing the work as "a children's tale of tolerance, compassion and diversity, written by Ben Ross Berenberg for his daughter. The recording features the voice of Ray Bolger, music composed by Alec Wilder, and a supporting cast of farm animals."[9]

SPOKEN WORD PUBLISHERS

Caedmon, the first publisher dedicated to recording spoken word literature, was founded by Barbara Cohen Holdridge and Marianne Roney in 1952. In a 2002 interview with Renee Montagne for National Public Radio, the pair recalled the recording session with poet Dylan Thomas that launched the company.

> Several missed recording studio appointments later, there stood Dylan Thomas, poems in hand. But not enough, it turned out, to fill a long-playing record. A catastrophe in the making, remembers Barbara Holdridge, since the B side had to have something on it, or they couldn't put out the record. They asked the poet if he had anything else he could record. Holdridge says: "He thought for a minute, and he said, 'Well, I did this story that was published in *Harper's Bazaar* that was a kind of Christmas story.'" It was "A Child's Christmas in Wales." They borrowed the only known file copy from the magazine. "That was dusting off something that undoubtedly would have remained buried and that became one of the most loved and popular stories recorded in the 20th century and certainly gave us the start that we needed to become a viable company," Holdridge says.[10]

The National Recording Registry noted the lasting importance of this captivating childhood remembrance in a citation for the recording: "It became one of Caedmon's most successful releases and has been credited with launching the audiobook industry in the United States."[11] Interestingly, in 1986 Caedmon was acquired by HarperCollins, a company that traces its roots back to the Bubble Books.

The year 1953 marked the launch of Weston Woods, the venerable children's film and audiobook producer that continues to publish award-winning titles more than a half-century after its first release, *Andy and the Lion.* Mort Schindel, the company founder, dedicated his life to translating the best in children's picture book literature into audiovisual media, fulfilling a role described as "teacher to millions."[12] Schindel's meticulous attention to every aspect of filmmaking included the creation of a soundtrack that integrated stellar narration, original music, and sound effects that enhanced a child's understanding of the story. The first incarnations of Weston Woods's audiobooks were vinyl LPs released under the series title *Read Me a Story* in 1959. The first series consisted of sixteen stories, four to a disc, containing the soundtrack of early Schindel films such as *Make Way for Ducklings, Mike Mulligan and His Steam Shovel,* and *Millions of Cats.* Later, the soundtracks to Weston Woods children's literature filmstrips were also released as audio-only cassette tapes. In 1987, Weston Woods developed entirely new readalong (book-plus-cassette) versions of previously released titles by remastering the original or rerecording a new soundtrack, with the resulting audiobooks—such as *Where the Wild Things Are*—distributed by Scholastic. From that point forward, as each film was produced, the soundtrack elements were reedited and mixed to make the audiobook version its own entity.[13] (Weston Woods was acquired by Scholastic in 1996.)

In 1955, Anthony Ditlow, a former teacher who was losing his eyesight, founded Listening Library in partnership with his wife, Helen. Ditlow combined his knowledge of Talking Books for the vision impaired with his awareness of the curricular needs of students by developing a list of spoken word titles marketed to schools and libraries, such as perennial young adult favorite *Lord of the Flies* narrated by author Sir William Golding. From its first production, *Around the World in Eighty Days,* to its first recording of a children's book in 1962, *Pippi Longstocking,* Listening Library built its reputation on providing an experience that Anthony Ditlow, on the packaging of his first LP recording in 1955, compared to "a personal friend reading aloud—flawlessly, tirelessly, and with dramatic feeling." The founders' son Tim Ditlow joined the firm in 1979, his expert ear selecting the best in children and young adult literature for unabridged recording, which soon became the firm's sole focus. Listening Library blazed new trails under the guidance of Tim Ditlow, named company president in 1986. Listening Library produced consumer editions of children's audiobooks meticulously faithful to the original text in full-color packaging, which were sold in Waldenbooks stores and released the first full-cast recordings of unabridged novels for children. It also instituted a lifetime replacement policy for library editions and pioneered the inclusion of bonus material such as author interviews and visual images on computer-playable discs. Listening Library's 1998 acquisition of *Harry Potter and the Sorcerer's Stone,* combined with Ditlow's casting of Jim Dale as narrator, resulted in a series that shattered all previous audiobook sales records. Part of the Random House Audio Publishing Group since 1999, the company continues its tradition of excellence into the twenty-first century, maintaining the high standards set by its founder. On Listening Library's behalf, Helen Ditlow accepted the Lifetime Achievement Award from the Audio Publishers Association in 2005.[14]

Lucien Adès broke new ground when he combined pop culture with children's recordings, developing record albums with attached readalong pages, which were based on licensed Walt Disney films. Adès originally developed his product in 1953 as a bookseller in Paris, and later established a marketing partnership of his Adès Editions label with the Walt Disney Productions French office.[15] In 1957, Disney brought the idea to the United States, releasing the first in the Storyteller line of LP albums that combined the songs and story adaptations of such films as *Bambi, Dumbo,* and *Pinocchio.* These recordings, with the cover slogan "See the pictures / Hear the record / Read the book," coached a generation of listeners in the how-to technique of readalong audiobooks with this phrase: "You can read along with me in your book. You will know it's time to turn the page when Tinker Bell rings her little bells like this . . . Let's begin now."[16]

FEDERAL SUPPORT

Children's audiobooks received support through Eisenhower-era federal programs that recognized the educational benefits of recorded literature envisioned by Edison in the previous century. The National Defense Act of 1958 provided grants for radio, television, film, and audiovisual media, thus contributing to the growth of children's audiobook production. The Elementary and Secondary Education Act of 1965, in effect through reauthorization for over forty subsequent years, was established to equalize educational opportunities for the disadvantaged, improve libraries, and provide programs for accelerated and struggling learners. These federal funds created an audiovisual boom in school libraries and classrooms, supplying students with new multimedia to enhance learning while transforming school librarians into media specialists. Audiobooks became an established part of literacy learning, whether as part of a readalong package or in the form of a filmstrip-and-cassette production. The strength of the school and library market for audiovisual adaptations of literature was such that in "1973 filmstrips with cassettes were the fastest growing media format in terms of commercial sales."[17]

TECHNOLOGICAL ADVANCES

New technologies revolutionized the way listeners experienced audiobooks and changed the audiobook-publishing playing field. The lull between the introduction of the long-playing record in 1948 and the introduction of the cassette tape by the Philips Corporation in 1963 soon gave way to a tsunami of competing formats.[18] Cassettes hastened the death of the LP and led to the demise of small independent companies that recorded children's literature on records. Gone were companies such as Newbery Award Records and Joseph Berk's one-man company Pathways to Sound, which in 1961 produced Jessica Tandy and Hume Cronyn reading *The Wind in the Willows,* Julie Harris narrating *Stuart Little* in 1965, and E. B. White reading his iconic *Charlotte's Web* in 1970[19] (after rejecting Berk's casting actress Hume for the recording, preferring to speak his own words without drama[20]). The availability of the cassette tape deck and the introduction of the Sony Walkman in 1979 revolutionized the audiobook world, allowing listeners to become mobile. After the brief mid-1960s lifespan of the eight-track tape, both portable and car cassette players became ubiquitous, making the cassette tape the dominant world format after two decades, outselling the vinyl LP by 1983.[21]

The rise of the cassette provided the technology that gave birth to Recorded Books, a company founded as a way for commuters to experience great books while behind the wheel. The shift from LP to cassettes led to a change in audiovisual hardware in the classroom, and tape players soon outnumbered turntables. Recorded Books recognized a new market and established a K–12 school division in the early 1990s with their first releases public domain children's classics, adding current best sellers and original educational content as the youth division grew.[22] Sony and Phillips jointly developed the compact disc in 1982, and Sony's first portable CD player was launched in 1984. A mere four years later, CD sales surpassed LP records, yet the cassette tape remained a viable audiobook format into the twenty-first century.[23] The new media formats stimulated growth in the audiobook publishing field, with the establishment of Live Oak Media in 1980, Blackstone Audio in 1987, Audio Bookshelf in 1992, Listen & Live Audio in 1997, and Full Cast Audio in 2001.

Digital audio players first appeared in 1997, and Apple's release of the iPod in 2001 marked the beginning of the MP3 era. Audiobooks quickly migrated to the digital format, with Audible.com developing the concept of download retail sales in 1995, and the first library download service, OverDrive, providing online checkout of audiobooks in 2002. All-in-one units—such as the Playaway, which debuted in 2005—offered the digital audiobook in a preloaded package that eliminated the need for CDs or playback unit. Whatever the container, twenty-first century audiobooks allow listeners to carry literature along in an ever-changing array of formats, transmuting the ageless appeal of storytelling into an outward form that echoes the prediction made in 1650 by the writer Cyrano de Bergerac:

> On opening a box, I discovered in it a metal object, not unlike one of our clocks, which was filled with all manner of tiny springs and mysterious machines. It was a book indeed, but a miraculous book, with neither pages nor letters; it was, in short, a book where the eyes were useless for reading and for which only the ears were needed. When someone desires to "read," he winds up this machine with a great quantity of little threads of all kinds, then he turns the needle to the chapter he wishes to hear and at once there issue from it, as from the mouth of a man or from a musical instrument, all the distinct and different sounds which the great lunarians employ for the expression of their language.[24]

SPOTLIGHT REFLECTION

A Good Story, Well Told BY PAUL GAGNE

LOOKING BACK OVER MY thirty-two-year history of working on children's recordings for Weston Woods Studios, I've observed some pretty significant changes in the audiobook world. I don't know if *audiobook* was even a standard term when I started as a sound editor in 1978. At the time I was only peripherally aware of some of the other producers doing book recordings—Caedmon, Listening Library, Books on Tape. I became more aware of the audiobook as its own entity when we started producing readalong recordings in the late 1980s, when we needed to go back and rerecord many of the titles in the Weston Woods catalog because the narrations for some of the older film soundtracks weren't always verbatim recordings of the text from the books.

I'd say one of the biggest changes I've noticed is that there is a far greater awareness of the audiobook as a respected art form, not only for me personally, but in the educational and consumer markets overall. And it's still growing, through the efforts of such organizations as the Audio Publishers Association, which formalized a community of audiobook producers and narrators; the Audio Publishers Association's Audie Awards; and the American Library Association's Odyssey Medal, which, in particular, has given the audiobook the kind of formal recognition and respect that motivates producers to strive for quality.

The other major change I've seen is in production technology. When I started in this field, recordings were done using reel-to-reel tape, and editing involved several weeks in a room with razor blades and splicing tape. Digital recording technology and computer applications have revolutionized all of that with easy-to-use, flexible tools that streamlined the editing, mixing, and mastering process from weeks to a matter of days, with no degradation of sound quality, resulting in equally flexible digital master files that can be converted to any of the digital formats currently in use—from an audio CD to downloadable MP3 files—with a few mouse clicks.

As the process of producing audiobooks has become easier and more flexible from a technology standpoint, we as producers have become freer to focus on the fundamentals that have always been at the heart of any good book recording. These are finding strong, well-told stories in the books we choose to adapt and casting readers with the kind of well-honed storytelling skills that can unlock and bring good literature to life for the listener.

Morton Schindel, the founder of Weston Woods, focused his original mission on finding the best literature for children, adapted as faithful reflections of the books themselves and preserving the integrity of the original. This is still very much at the heart of what we do at Weston Woods, and I think that any producer doing quality work in the audiobook field today has their focus on content rather than container. The more things have changed technologically, the more they've remained the same in terms of what lies at the foundation of any successful audiobook recording—a good story, well told.

Paul Gagne is the director of production at
Weston Woods/Scholastic Audio.

NOTES

1. Paul Henry Saenger, Space between Words: The Origins of Silent Reading (Stanford: Stanford University Press, 1997): 243.

2. "The Telephone," The Thomas Edison Papers, Rutgers University, http://edison.rutgers.edu/NamesSearch/SingleDoc.php3?DocId= SM029074.

3. "Mary Had a Little Lamb by Thomas Edison" (MP3 audio file), Project Gutenberg, www.gutenberg.org/ebooks/10137.

4. U.S. Government Printing Office, H.R. 4846 Engrossed Amendment Senate (EAS), October 25, 2000, www.gpo.gov/fdsys/pkg/BILLS -106hr4846eas/html/BILLS-106hr4846eas.htm.

5. "The National Recording Registry 2003," National Recording Preservation Board of the Library of Congress, www.loc.gov/rr/ record/nrpb/registry/nrpb-2003reg.html.

6. Merle Sprinzen, "Little Wonder Records and Bubble Books," accessed May 24, 2012, www.littlewonderrecords.com/index.html.

7. "NLS: That All May Read," National Library Service for the Blind and Physically Handicapped, Library of Congress, March 30, 2011, www.loc.gov/nls/about_history.html.

8. Peter Muldavin, The Complete Guide to Vintage Children's Records Identification and Value Guide, (Paducah KY: Collector Books, 2007).

9. "The Sounds of American Life and Legend Are Tapped for the Seventh Annual National Recording Registry," Library of Congress, June 25, 2009, www.loc.gov/today/pr/2009/09-108.html.

10. Renee Montagne, "Caedmon: Recreating the Moment of Inspiration Label Brought Words of Dylan Thomas, Other Writers to Life," NPR, December 5, 2002, www.npr.org/templates/story/story .php?storyId=866406.

11. The Full National Recording Registry, Library of Congress, www.loc.gov/rr/record/nrpb/registry/nrpb-masterlist.html.

12. John Cech, Imagination and Innovation: The Story of Weston Woods (New York: Scholastic, 2009).

13. Paul Gagne, in discussion with the author, February 8, 2009.

14. Tim Ditlow, in discussion with the author, January 22, 2011.

15. "Lucien Adès Bio," Disney, http://disney.go.com/disneyinsider/ history/legends/lucien-ades.

16. Tim Hollis and Greg Ehrbar, *Mouse Tracks: The Story of Walt Disney Records* (Jackson: University Press of Mississippi, 2006).

17. "In the 20th Century: A Brief History," Association for Educational Communications and Technology, www.aect.org/About/History/.

18. "An Audio Timeline: 1997," Audio Engineering Society, www.aes.org/aeshc/docs/audio.history.timeline.html.

19. Tom Long, "Joseph P. Berk, 77, of Cambridge; Gave Voice to Children's Classic Books," *Boston Globe* (March 16, 2004): C 10.

20. E. B. White, *Letters of E.B. White Revised Edition,* ed. by Dorothy Lobrano Guth. Revised and updated by Martha White (New York: Harper Collins, 2007), 548.

21. Meagan Haire, "A Brief History of the Walkman," *Time,* July 1, 2009, www.time.com/time/nation/article/0,8599,1907884,00.html.

22. Troy Juliar, in discussion with the author, February 1, 2011.

23. Toby Sterling, "Compact Disc Celebrates 25th Anniversary," *USA Today,* August 17, 2007, www.usatoday.com/tech/news/techinnovations/2007-08-16-compact-disc-anniversary_N.htm.

24. Cyrano de Bergerac, *Other Worlds: The Comical History of the States and Empires of the Moon and of the Sun,* trans. by Geoffrey Strachan (London: Oxford University Press, 1965), 88–89.

2 What Is an Audiobook? Why Listen?

WHAT EXACTLY IS AN audiobook? At its core, it is a spoken word recording of a work of literature. Most audiobooks stem from a printed text, read aloud by a narrator. The growing popularity of the audiobook genre has created an eager audience for an assortment of styles and variations on the spoken word theme. Notable narrators build an enthusiastic fan base with each new recording. Dedicated listeners become connoisseurs of a publisher's recognizable style, developing a personal preference for a company's consistent production characteristics of narration techniques, track length standards, background effects, use of music, and more. How do these characteristics combine to create an exceptional production? And why should children and young adults expand their appreciation of literature with audiobooks?

THE NARRATION

A key factor in audiobook excellence is the narrator, who delivers the author's words to the listener through the power of the spoken word. Occasionally a book's author may serve as the narrator, or the publisher might cast a celebrity to read a work. More commonly, a seasoned voice actor serves as narrator, knowledgeable in the techniques of communicating the author's intention through audible emotion and expression. The audiobook's executive producer evaluates talent through audition and casts voices who match the age, gender, setting, era, and mood of the book. Next, the audiobook director and narrator agree upon a narration style. A book may be read as a *single-voiced* narration, where the narrator uses his natural voice in a straightforward style that conveys changing characters through pacing and intonation, with little or no variation from the natural voice. In a *fully voiced* narration, a solo voice actor creates a unique tone and timbre for each character, employing changes in pitch and tempo, in addition to using her natural voice. The narration might be a mix of single-voiced and fully voiced, where the majority of the book is performed as a straight read in the natural voice, with major or pivotal characters marked by vocal differentiation; this style is sometimes termed *partially voiced.*

A book may call for a cast of two or more readers to communicate the author's intent. For example, a book that is split into parts may be produced as a *multivoiced* audiobook, with different narrators reading each section, but not necessarily an actor for each character or recorded at the same time. A book that is voiced by multiple readers performing as individual characters during an ensemble reading is a *fully cast* production, where the text of the book remains intact with the occasional removal of "he said," "she said" attributives. An audio *dramatization,* reminiscent of radio theater, is usually multivoiced, often with sound effects and music, and may include alteration of the original text or be an audio original.

THE CORE CONTENT

Children's and young adult audiobooks are most commonly *unabridged* recordings, where each word of the work's original text is read by the narrator, with the occasional deletion of front or end matter such as the appendix. The term *abridged* signals an audiobook that has been condensed and edited by a professional abridger with the author's permission, remaining true to the spirit and content of book. Adult audiobooks are often recorded in both abridged and unabridged versions, but this is unusual in youth titles. Audiobooks packaged with the original picture book are *readalong* productions. Readalongs are intended to be perused by a child who listens with the book in hand, experiencing the audiobook's narration, music, and sound effects in conjunction with the text and illustrations. The ease and availability of digital recording has resulted in the *audio original,* where a work is either released solely as an audio production having never appeared in print, or recorded and released prior to publication of the print title. Some audiobooks have *bonus material* or *enhanced content,* where the production contains not only the original text but also supplementary material such as an author interview or images from the print edition. The combination of expert narration and an appropriate production style result in an audiobook that allows the listener to experience the power of story through twenty-first century media.

THE IMPACT ON LITERACY

From the beginning, story served as a way to communicate an alternate reality, to build an imaginary world in the mind through sound and symbol. Humans use visual and aural means to convey information, telling tales through storytelling, art, music, and written language. The desire for story has inspired artists to seek multiple means to create their images, employing the art and technology of the age. Each has its own way of impacting the senses; each employs the brain in unique ways. Literacy is the ability to translate these media messages into our personal interpretation of the story. Every person has a natural learning style, a connection to one medium or another; yet all can develop skills to appreciate and understand the story in whatever method is used. Audiobooks communicate through sound, requiring a different set of literacy skills than print media, yet engaging many of the same comprehension skills as reading.

Audiobooks are a powerful tool in building fluency, the ability to read smoothly and expressively. Expert narration provides listeners with a model of how proficient readers process meaning in complete phrases, rather than word-by-word, turning printed punctuation into nuanced pause and emphasis. And listening to audiobooks boosts pronunciation skills: young children can see the link between sound and symbol in a readalong, while older listeners hear words they know by sight spoken correctly. Vocabulary is increased as unknown words are encountered within fluidly spoken context, the meaning revealed by the narrator's tone. Audiobooks allow the listener to concentrate on the work's theme, conflict, setting, and character development while making mental predictions about the story's outcome, removing the struggle of decoding text and fostering engagement in the story while developing critical thinking skills. Struggling readers may find that following along in the text while listening provides a path to comprehension, or they may be liberated through listening by itself, later returning to the book with the memory of the fluid narration to help their own reading.

The unique qualities of an audiobook promote important active listening skills. Audiobooks ground the listener in the here-and-now, with no flipping back a page or skimming forward. Children who listen to literature build auditory stamina and focus, which are critical language arts competencies. A person's listening comprehension is at least two years above their reading comprehension, providing all listeners with material that stretches their intellectual capacity. Gifted readers, who devour text so quickly they can miss literary nuance, cannot rush an audiobook and learn to slow down to savor details overlooked while reading.

When reading text, we filter the author's words through a personal internal voice, allowing our own gender, age, and background to color our literary experience. Audiobooks remove this filter, allowing a listener to more fully connect with the essence of the book's emotional core. Audiobooks open an existential doorway, providing listeners a direct connection to unfamiliar customs, eras, ethnicities, and events through a production that expands meaning through authentic vocal casting and evocative background music. This same attention to accents and dialects, as well as regional and cultural vocal patterns, allows listeners from marginalized communities to hear their own reality mirrored in literature.

Audiobooks build a literary community open to all, providing a common experience for conversation and intellectual exploration among English-language learners, those with learning disabilities, gifted students, and reluctant readers. Commercially produced audiobooks as well as resources available through both Learning Ally (formerly Recording for the Blind and Dyslexic) and the National Library Service for the Blind and Physically Handicapped provide recordings to those with print disabilities. Access to audiobooks increases exposure to literature beyond a child's independent reading level, allowing families to share literature together, forging a lifelong love of reading. Classrooms integrate audiobooks in language arts instruction, expanding students' multimedia literacy while incorporating cultural understanding. A growing body of research validates the importance of audiobooks in education (see appendix B, "Recommended Reading"). In 1985, the Commission on Reading declared, "The single most important activity for building the knowledge required for eventual success in reading is reading aloud to children."[1] Expertly produced and narrated audiobooks provide this key factor to success, through an experience that re-creates the visceral pleasure of "Once upon a time . . ."

SPOTLIGHT REFLECTION

Love of Literature through Listening
BY BRUCE COVILLE

THE LIFE OF THE senses starts with sound.

The first thing we experience in the womb, before we see, before we smell, before we taste anything, is sound, the human voice of our mothers and our fathers. And because we start by hearing, it's no wonder that the human voice has such profound power and impact on us, that we long for its sound, and that it is the medium that carries story to us most effectively.

For years there has been an issue, a question, about how seriously we can take the audiobook field. Isn't it cheating to *hear* a story rather than read it? I propose that if you give children a great story experience, they'll come willingly into the world of books and literature. Those of us who love this field—educators, producers, performers—have been preaching for years about the pedagogical value of the audiobook format.

Stories are the most powerful teaching tool we have. And one thing they teach, in a way that's impossible by any other method, is empathy. We are a vast and diverse culture in danger of flying apart at the seams. The one capacity that stitches us all together is empathy, the ability to put yourself inside the skin of another human being. And the only way to teach that skill to children is through story, story that grabs them and puts them inside someone else's life.

But beyond all the educational value is the fact that *kids just need stories.*

I fell in love with audiobooks more than twenty years ago, on a six-week, cross-country trip with my 14-year-old daughter. We went to the library to get audiobooks because, at that time, the library was the only place where you could find unabridged titles. As our brand-new rental car had no cassette player, we brought along a boom box and she held it in her lap—plugged into the cigarette lighter—all the way across the country. I learned two powerful things on this trip. One: When you're driving through Kansas, *Pride and Prejudice* is riveting. Two: When you listen together, you have a shared literary experience unlike any other.

I love being read to, and I love reading aloud. But when you do that one person is in charge. When you listen to an audiobook with someone else, you receive it at the same time. You can't skip ahead. You can't find out what's going on. One person doesn't know. You experience it together. Audiobooks are the great equalizer. Kids who can't read the book can hear the audiobook, so all the kids in the classroom can be talking about the same thing. They can have that shared experience.

To the question "Is it cheating to listen to a book instead of read it?" my response is, "What is the point of connecting children and books to begin with?" Is it to insist that someone slog through a hundred pages of text? Or is it to make sure that a child has had a meaningful experience with a piece of literature? We move more deeply into literature when we hear it. Was it cheating to listen to Shakespeare? Would it have been cheating to listen to Homer sing *The Odyssey*? Families used to gather together to read. Were they cheating?

Let us hear it. Let us hear the sound of the author's voice. Books were made to be shared in this way. Audiobooks are not just a wave of the future, they're the *sound* wave of the future.

Bruce Coville is a former educator, prolific
author, and founder of Full Cast Audio.

NOTES

1. Richard Allan, et al., Becoming a Nation of Readers: The Report of the Commission on Reading (Washington, D.C.: The National Institute of Education, 1985).

3 The Art of the Audiobook

Setting the Stage, Speaking the Page

AN AUTHOR VIEWS HIS published book as the cumulating form of artistic endeavor, yet that same work serves as the rough draft of an audiobook production. The best in recorded literature begins with the printed word and, through an ensemble of efforts, reflects and reshapes the text into an expressive new medium. Audiobooks are not merely texts read aloud into a microphone. There's a whole host of behind-the-scenes creative artists involved in the production. Through a series of interviews, we'll follow the creation of an audiobook by highlighting the roles of each individual who adds their imprint on the final production.

AUDIOBOOK ACQUISITION

We begin our travels on the path of production with Rebecca Waugh, senior acquisitions editor at Listening Library, as she discusses the process of selecting titles for production as audiobooks. "Listening to an audiobook feels like reading to me," she says, "so I search for the same qualities that I look for in a good book. Sometimes I'm looking for books that will stretch kids a little and make them think. Other times I'm looking for books that will make fun, easy listening. The major difference from print books is that it's even more important to have a strong story, one that will engage kids' attention fully, make them care about the characters and what happens to that character. The common thread among all the books that we turn into audiobooks is that the writing is strong enough to stand the test of being read out loud."

Yet audiobook acquisition must match the realities of the publisher's business model and listener demands. Waugh describes how she must keep in mind production and sales when selecting upcoming productions: "Every season we publish about thirty titles, and I'm looking for a selection of titles that is broad enough to include young children, mid-grade tweens, and teen listeners. Even within those groups, kids can have very different interests. Sometimes I aim for the middle and look for a book that a broad spectrum of listeners can enjoy. Or I'll come across a book that I adore and I feel will resonate for a specific kind of listener." Usually the acquisitions editor relies on the producer to cast the recording at a later stage, but occasionally a manuscript has strong creative potential, such as music or sound effects, enhanced content, a particular narrator, or even multiple narrators. Then Waugh may include the executive producer in the process early on, to read the manuscript and brainstorm ideas and get a sense of how to translate the work into a new medium.

Listening Library is owned by Random House; such production companies may have first pick of the parent company's print titles. Most audiobook publishers meet regularly with literary agents or book editors to evaluate upcoming releases; or an audiobook acquisitions editor may see an intriguing print deal and approach the author's agent. Waugh attends the Bologna Children's Book Fair each year to meet with publishers and editors from around the world. She explains, "While in Bologna, everyone does a lot of talking, and then we go home to actually start reading. I take a nonscientific approach and try to get a sense of the trends, what people are excited about. I never buy a title without having read it or having someone in our department read it."

No matter the author or print publisher, the acquisitions editor must create a varied sales list. Waugh explains her balancing act: "There are a number of authors who have a history with Listening Library, and we tend to feel loyalty toward them. Though it's true that some writers are so prolific we can't necessarily publish everything they write on audio. Listening

Library was an independent publisher of children's audiobooks for fifty years before acquisition by Random House, so we also continue a tradition of keeping a diverse list and publishing works from other houses."

Changing business and production models allow audiobooks to be produced much more quickly than in the past. Waugh notes, "In general, I try to find good titles and acquire them early enough so that the audiobook can be published simultaneously with the print version. This matters the most for really popular titles, because an audio listener is going to want to be able to listen when the book is released. But being simultaneous isn't always essential. Reviews matter a lot in children's publishing, and certainly I've seen some titles sell better a year after publication because of an ALA award or through word of mouth. If I hear about an overlooked gem, I'll give it a look and decide if it would make a good audiobook. Classics are a thriving part of our backlist too, because these are stories that adults recognize, and they know that they'll enjoy situations where the entire family will be listening together."

The impact of new methods of publishing and changing distribution rights hasn't revolutionized audiobook publishing from an acquisitions perspective. As Waugh reflects, "Going digital hasn't changed the way I acquire titles—at least, not yet. I think the main challenge in going digital is figuring out where we fit in with enhanced e-books and apps. Although e-books have been around for a while, it's easy to see that there's potential to be creative with bonus features and audio in enhanced digital formats."[1]

PRODUCTION AND DIRECTION

As the audiobook moves into the recording studio, a new team takes charge of the production. I spoke with David Rapkin, a Grammy and Audie award–winning independent audiobook producer and director. As he explains it, "A producer or executive producer is involved with the budget and the gathering of all of the pieces of the production puzzle. The executive producer will hire the director, book the recording studio, and arrange for postproduction and sound mastering. The producer is responsible for the dispersing of the budget and the deep background knowledge of the personnel needed to do the job and is generally responsible for all of the deadlines. If there's a problem you can go and knock on the producer's door, because it's his or her responsibility to make sure that all of these ducks are in a row."

Rapkin is best known for his work on many touchstone audio productions, including the Harry Potter audiobook series. He details how excellence in audiobook production begins long before the narrator enters the recording booth: "As a director, I spend many more hours working on preparation for the book than I do recording it. The director focuses his concentration on the job of knowing everything there is to know about the script—the book to be recorded. A good director should go into a recording session knowing how to answer any question that is being asked about the script, such as pronunciations and historical references, things contextual within the story that give you a sense of social framework and the character's attitude. Another crucial role of the director is to make the meaning of the text arise though a subtle thing like emphasis. Emphasis can change everything. I submit to you that there is a qualitative difference between groundhog meat and ground *hog* meat. They're two different things.

"My directions will take usually about ten seconds, in as brief language as possible so that the energy of the session will not be lost. I never interrupt an actor. My process is one where we do two pages at a time. At the end of those two pages we'll go back, we'll do pickups—rerecord errors—and we'll move on. But I never interrupt an actor, because that ruins the state of mind that the actor must get in and frustrates their ability to create a dramatic line. There are story lines within sentences, within paragraphs, within chapters, within books. If those arcs are not observed it will be a piecemeal production and the listener will say 'I'm not interested anymore . . . this is not a very good audiobook . . . it didn't keep my attention.' That's because the magic, the thrall, is ruined."

Audiobook listeners benefit from this attention to crafting an aural literary experience, allowing complete immersion in the author's world. But what about terms and phrases unique to the work, such as the invented world of Harry Potter? Rapkin says that's a good example, "because in the beginning I could call Jo Rowling up and ask her. But there are many layers between a lowly audio producer and a much-exalted celebrity writer. I use my sense of language context to explicate the pronunciation of names if the author is unavailable or if it is a last minute title and we must go in and do the best we can."

And does Rapkin feel that there is a difference in directing audiobooks for young adults or children compared to adult titles? He explains, "In audiobooks for young people, it's important to imbue the production with a sense of innocent excitement, without an adult sensibility, in the way the actor approaches reading the book and the characters. It's a very delicate kind of energy that is easily extinguished if ham-handed adultness is permitted to enter the process. It has to do with a lightness of voice. It has to do with a kind of enthusiasm. It has to do with keeping emotions close to the surface. In an adult book many things can be implied, but in a young person's audiobook the subtlety can be relaxed so that the feelings can emerge."

Once listeners have become connoisseurs of the art of audiobook, their attuned ears will recognize the stellar facets of a top-notch production. But what about a title where even a neophyte can tell that the narrator wasn't the best choice for the job? Rapkin notes, "You've put your finger on something central to the entire process: if there were such a thing as 'the world's best actor,' and this 'world's best actor' were miscast, nothing would save the production. I would say that 80 percent of the director's responsibility is in casting correctly. If it's miscast, all you can do is damage control. That doesn't mean that the narrator is bad; it means that the reader is miscast. There are many very talented actors who are wonderful but can't read audiobooks. It's not because they're illiterate; it's because reading audiobooks is a very specialized kind of craft and not everyone can do it. I like to compare audiobook production to musical performance. We've all experienced a note-perfect concert that has no soul, yet we've also experienced a performance where there were a few clams but it was so at the heart of the music that it didn't matter that they struck some wrong notes. It didn't matter one whit. It wasn't letter-perfect, but it was soul-perfect. My aim is to create that soul-stirring audiobook." [2]

It's true that many productions will have forgivable flaws, while maintaining mesmerizing brilliance. Yet listeners can be pulled out of the production's enchantment by a disconcerting distraction, such as the mangling of a word. Paul Topping, director of research at Recorded Books, holds a unique position in the audiobook world, providing linguistic guidance for the world's largest independent publisher of unabridged audiobooks. Topping began his career at the American Foundation for the Blind in 1983 as a Studio Monitor. He remembers, "My responsibilities included proofreading and directing the production of Talking Books, the AFB productions for the National Library Service for the Blind and Physically Handicapped. In those days, narrators spent hours conducting their own research in the reference room of the AFB studios as well as on the phone, consulting the authors whose books they were narrating. We studio monitors would work with them in the booth, at the same time directing, running the tape recorders, and looking up pronunciations in dictionaries and other reference works. At the end of those two-hour recording sessions we studio monitors would proofread—really proof-listen—to each others' tapes. In short, it was our job to find errors."

In his current position, Topping has established methods to facilitate language research. He describes how the process has integrated both old and new technologies: "When I went to work for Recorded Books in 1994, the first change that I made was to implement a unified pronunciation key, as all American dictionaries use a different pronunciation notation. Over the course of the past years, we've been availing ourselves of the mind-boggling, ever-expanding body of information available on the Internet. But with great discretion. There is much misinformation on the Web. Online dictionaries and databases are rife with errors, and you also have to be very choosy when relying on websites that provide audio clips of pronunciations provided by 'native speakers.' But there are great benefits [to using the Internet] as well. There are wonderful forums such as wordreference.com where linguists can discuss pronunciation and translation issues. There are video sites where a researcher can hear an individual pronouncing his or her own name, as well as jargon whose pronunciation needs to be clarified. Best of all, the Internet allows us to do something we could never do before with print media alone: cross-checking."

Topping shares a fascinating story about linguistic detective work that combined old-fashioned library research with Internet resources. "We were about to record *The Jungle Book* by Rudyard Kipling. I had instinctual doubts that I could trust the pronunciations used in the Disney version. I looked far and wide in reference works dealing with literature and drew a blank. I then turned to the Internet to see if I could find a glossary of characters for this work. I didn't, but I did learn two things. Firstly, that Kipling's widow was unhappy with Disney's pronunciation of 'Mowgli' and attempted to sue them (in vain, alas) when they wouldn't correct it. Secondly, that Kipling included a pronouncing glossary of *The Jungle Book* available in only one of its many editions. Within seconds I was able to request an interlibrary loan, and within two days I had it in my hands. There was much production debate, though. Should we present our listeners with a version of *The Jungle Book* with the familiar Disney pronunciations, or should we take the high road and stay true to the author's intended pronunciations? We ultimately chose the latter, but it was not without much deliberation and general hand-wringing and brow-mopping."

When asked if even the youngest audiobook listener should be the beneficiary of careful research, Topping replies, "Absolutely! Effective pronunciation research leads to language learning—one of the prime benefits of audiobook listening, no matter the age. Meticulous production in the audiobook industry includes linguistic accuracy. If we employ only one form of research, we are doing a great disservice to our listeners. An audiobook shouldn't be thrown together quickly in someone's garage. It should be crafted carefully, with passion and great attention to detail."[3]

THE ART OF NARRATION

It's clear that many professionals are involved along the creative path, each adding their expertise to the audiobook. The essential role of narrator is key to the production, with the best voice actors able to remove the wall of performance, drawing the listener fully into the literary experience. Katherine Kellgren—named *Booklist*'s 2011 "Voice of Choice" and winner of multiple honors and awards for her voicing of adult, young adult, and children's audiobooks—gives an insider's look at the role of audiobook narration.

Audiobook fans often wonder how actors break into the narration field. American-born Kellgren, who studied acting at the London Academy of Music and Dramatic Art, found her first professional audiobook acting job as a last-minute fill-in. But it's clear that her lifelong love of recorded literature plus extraordinary talent and dedication are the qualities that have led to her success, with over 150 productions to her credit. When queried about how she handles her career, Kellgren replies, "I have an agent, but I have also made demo recordings with three or four two-minute samples of work I have done on previous books and send them out to different publishers. I attend industry events like Audio Publishers Association Conferences and mixers to keep in touch with producers. Another valuable resource is social networking, which allows narrators to keep in touch with industry professionals and listeners alike. The world of audiobooks is a relatively tight-knit community, with even fewer major producers than the worlds of theater or film, so once a narrator is established, they tend to be approached by companies more frequently. But it can take years to establish relationships, and it is a rare narrator who has worked with every major producer."

Regarding her preparation before a recording session, Kellgren says, "I have a fairly elaborate method of marking up and preparing text. As I read, I go through and write anything descriptive the author has stated, such as 'he said sulkily' or 'she said excitedly' in the margins, as well as looking up the pronunciations of words. I will often do an online image search if the author is describing something in detail that I haven't seen, such as a type of flower or a famous building, so I can picture it when I'm reading. I try and find the tunes to any songs the author is referencing and study any accents that are used, sometimes working with a dialect or singing coach if I feel unsure of what I'm doing. Then I go through and highlight the dialogue of every character in a different color. I'll do this with a paper copy, or I often have the book as a PDF on my iPad and digitally mark text by using color highlighting and annotation apps."

Kellgren also shares how she "casts" the character voices she will use and how she creates and retains the accuracy of her voicings: "I am a voracious listener of audiobooks and recordings of plays on audio. As a child and young adult, I obsessively listened to a large collection of Caedmon recordings of authors reading their own work—a favorite was Tennessee Williams—as well all-cast recordings of classic plays featuring great actors such as John Gielgud and Edith Evans. I draw on the voices from these recordings, as well as actors from current film and stage—not to mention family members and people I hear on the bus. When portraying a British character, I draw on my study of regional dialects of Great Britain for three years during my drama training. When I do a sequel or a series, I write down any characters that recur as I read through the book, and then take a digital sample of how I voice each character using a sound editing program on my computer. Then I make a 'character playlist' in iTunes that I can refer to when recording subsequent books."

Asked to describe a typical audiobook recording, Kellgren notes, "The session lasts usually from 10 a.m. until 4 or 6 p.m., with short breaks during the day as well as a lunch break. It can be fairly exhausting, as you can't let your concentration wander for even a moment because it will be reflected in the finished product. As a more practiced narrator, I can gener-ally record between eighty and one hundred fifty pages per day, depending on how dense the text is—sometimes more if the book is not being edited in the 'punch and roll' style while being recorded, which involves a lot of starting and stopping to rerecord errors. The importance of a great sound editor is immeasurable, making the sometimes stumbling work of many hours seem to fly by seamlessly for the listener."

Does Kellgren ever worry about beginning a series and not being able to complete it? She admits, "I do sometimes worry about this. In my first years as a narrator, a case in point would be the Araminta Spookie series by Angie Sage. After I did the first two (recorded two at a time because they are short), I pined away, checking Amazon periodically to see if any other books in this series had been published and praying that I would be asked to do them. When I finally got to record numbers 3 and 4 as audio-books, one can only imagine my joy! But there is still a fifth book left in the series, and to this day I still sometimes find myself staring at the ceiling at 3 a.m. thinking about it. I've gone on to record many children's and YA series, and life can be very complicated and worrying, as sequel production all depends on sales of earlier titles."

Kellgren has her favorites among her work. "I loved every minute of narrating the Jacky Faber series by L. A. Meyer, produced by Listen & Live Audio, which received Odyssey Honor recognitions by the American Library Association. During the recording, I tracked down over forty folk songs and sea shanties, whose tunes I had to sing accurately, working with a singing coach in different keys for both male and female characters. I portray various characters with different dialects, from a drunken Scots-man to a Cockney tavern performer, a bashful naval officer, and a chorus of prim nineteenth-century Boston schoolgirls. I even tracked down a web-site with animal sound clips when I needed to voice a laugh described as 'the snort of an evil-minded camel.' Every bit as fun as it sounds!"[4]

Audiobook accolades depend on the expertise of the director and produc-tion team, as well as the vocal acrobatics of such conscientious narrators as Katherine Kellgren, all essential on the path of production. But just as the essentials of the print publishing world have shifted radically in the digital age, so too has audio publishing. The impact of new technology can best be seen once the postproduction team goes into action. The path to audiobook excellence has some new and interesting twists as we move from the procuring and performance of the author's words into the realm of editing and distributing the final production.

NOTES

1. Rebecca Waugh, in discussion with the author, July 8, 2010.
2. David Rapkin, in discussion with the author, July 27, 2010.
3. Paul Topping, in discussion with the author, July 30, 2010.
4. Katherine Kellgren, in discussion with the author, August 5, 2010.

4 Continuing the Path to Production

Editing, Marketing,
and the Creativity of Business

IN CHAPTER 3, WE explored how the audiobook production team selects a literary work and reinterprets it in audio format. The roles of acquisition editor, producer, director, researcher, and narrator have remained much the same since the time of vinyl records. As new methods and techniques enter the marketplace, the audiobook process and product are both altered and modified, with digital technology blazing new paths and leading audio publishers into uncharted territory.

A CHANGING BUSINESS MODEL

Laura Colebank is cofounder and partner of Tantor Audio, an audiobook company founded in 2000. She describes the company's business model and how digital recording, emerging technologies, and new economies have changed the world of audiobook publishing. When asked how her company locates, acquires, and produces over fifty new titles a month, she points out that according to Audible, in 2009, 90,000 print titles (excluding textbooks, research, and cookbooks) were published, but only 5,000 released as audiobooks. "So there is a large pool of titles to research and consider," she says. "At Tantor, it's a combined effort involving our licensing team, management and sales. We have developed a Tantor 'mining' system that involves multiple resources and specific criteria."

The company tries to strike a balance between simultaneous new releases, classics, and YA titles, Colebank says. "Our simultaneous releases of front-list titles are about 70 percent of the titles that we publish. We do record many classic public domain titles—one might think these would be the easiest to obtain and publish, yet there can be twenty to thirty versions available, so our licensing department spends time researching which version is the highest in demand. Many of these classic titles cross over into the YA category, and we include a companion PDF e-book with classics to expand the educational market. We are always looking for YA titles that will appeal to both adults and teens—new series in particular, as they are popular among our teenage listeners."

Colebank notes that there are specific qualities of a print work to look for. "The flow of a book is key. If it's a page turner and we can't put a book down, we know we've found a title that will transfer extremely well into an audio format. If the book jumps around between present and future, or from one character to another; if there are a lot of quotes or footnotes, it will not be well suited for audio. While we occasionally publish titles which include charts and graphs that are found within the book's print edition, we make sure it flows even if a listener can't refer to the additional material."

Tantor Media has been an innovator in the incorporation of digital technology and recording methods, tweaking the models of producer, director, narrator and sound engineer, and establishing in-home self-recording of narrators. Colebank says, "Our company's audiobook software allows narrators to record books off-site or in their own home. The process begins with a narrator's research—reading the book, researching the book, corresponding with the author regarding questionable pronunciations, dialects, and nuances. The software allows narrators to record at their own pace, with the actual recording typically taking double the amount of time of a finished audiobook. However, the total time of the process is much longer once the narrator's research is taken into account. Once the narration is complete, the finished audio is downloaded to Tantor's audio department. Our proofing team compares the spoken text with the written word to verify that it matches perfectly. If any audio sections need rerecording, these pickups are sent to the narrator, who rerecords the segments. The audiobook passes one final round of proofing, and we have our final master—the audiobook. The recording is then manufactured and packaged in our warehouse and distributed within days."

Colebank says that staying on the cutting edge of technology gives audiobook publishers benefits in cost and production, "Advances in technology have allowed us the efficiencies that make it possible to publish a larger number of titles every month. As digital sales grow and hard good sales decrease, there will be increased savings, the biggest being no returns from retailers. Efficiencies in the recording and mastering process must continue to improve as pricing models have moved from higher-priced library editions to lower-priced downloads. It will be interesting to see how the library download market will shake out. Will authors receive higher royalties for higher circulating titles to compensate for the lower-priced downloads?"

Colebank also reflects on the benefits of Web-based marketing. "We are embracing social media to connect with narrators, authors, libraries, and every audiobook lover out there. Not only do we want to spread the word about our latest, we also want to know what people would like from us. Are there certain services that a library is in need of when adding to their audiobook collection? Do fans want us to publish a particular title? Social media provides the perfect forum for discussion and gives us the opportunity to listen and respond accordingly. Young adults are referred to as the online generation—and with good reason. They have embraced new technology and are using multiple media tools, often simultaneously. In order to reach this audience, you have to be where they are. As we acquire more YA titles, we are looking at other ways to reach them, including blogs, YouTube videos, viral marketing, and word of mouth."[1]

POSTPRODUCTION PRECISION

After the narrator has left the studio, the postproduction team polishes the recording, removing errors and adding enhancements. Todd Hobin, a musician, composer, and sound engineer, divulges the secrets of digital editing and the role of a sound editor: "The advent of digital recording changed the way we think of editing. It's still tricky, but not as tedious as it used to be with razor and tape splicing of analog tapes. Now, when you hear a click, pop or gurgle you can visually zoom in on your computer screen and see the part of the sonic wave that's the anomaly—it sticks out like a sore thumb to the trained eye. If you're careful, you can remove it without taking away any of the word you want to keep. In most instances it's a matter of just how much care you want to expend, and what the budget will allow."

While other members of the audiobook production team work together, the engineer often works solo. "Sound editing is a lonely job," Hobin says. "We take three independent editorial passes of a recording in the sound studio, refining the accuracy and sound quality, before we pass it on to the check listener, who serves as the final proof editor. The first editor will edit for content, making sure all of the dialog and segments recorded at different times are in order and placed on a sound time line in the digital editing software. The next editor will adjust the pacing and clean up the sound. This is where we remove out-of-place noises and add or subtract periods of silence. The final pass is to listen for anything we might have missed, drop in music or other sound effects, set the inaudible tracks breaks, and create a finished master CD."

Rather than a hard-and-fast production schedule, Hobin's work flow is somewhat unique. "I work primarily with Full Cast Audio, in a collaboration that's not the norm for most audiobook productions. We take whatever time it takes to make it right. A great narrator can save you time in the editing studio. A big cast of voices can slow you down. How much music you create can also impact the time commitment. But my studio production partner, Brett Hoban, has some rules of thumb for how much time you can expect for a project with a brilliant narrator. How long does it take to produce a four-hour audiobook? It will take most of eight hours to record an expert voice actor. It should take an about equal amount of time, another eight hours, to edit. Then half that—an additional four hours—to add the final touches to create the master: twenty total hours in the studio for a four-hour production. The complete process usually takes five times the finished length of an audio—and that's to record a title with a single top-notch narrator."

Hobin wears more than one hat in the recording studio. "In a Full Cast Audio production, we compose original music for many projects. I suppose it would be a whole lot easier to drop in a little music from our purchased sound library. A sound library can be licensed through many music services that will lease or sell ready-made instrumental music beds for this purpose—that's why you might hear the same introductory theme on audiobooks from various companies. However, creating the perfect original underscore enhances the experience, so that's what we do. A great book calls out for a specific type of music with certain instrumentation. It's part of creating the environment that the characters live in. To do them justice, we feel that we must create for the listener that specific environment. If you're listening to a story that takes place in an Elizabethan castle, you should hear a medieval ensemble as the underscore."

Hoban explains, "I create music that fits the scene thematically, and just as important, it is written to match the exact length of the scene. I even like to insert little musical figures in between sentences to reflect the character's intentions. Music should support the dialogue. It should not detract from the story or overpower the characters. I feel that when I do my job right, you don't even know that I'm there. You may find yourself crying or delirious with joy because you're caught up in the story. Music enforces those feelings and helps keep you in the moment."

At the time of our interview in 2011, Hoban reflected on coming changes. "Currently, CDs are the medium and MP3 files are standard, but we are perched on the tipping point. In sound engineering, we use all kinds of software on different platforms and jump between them—so we are used to change and are able to adapt. The next big paradigm shift will be in delivery standards. Higher-quality audio is going to demand larger bandwidth. Downloads will be the standard delivery mechanism. Streaming audio will eventually rule. There is a recurring theme I see being played out during changing economies—time versus money. The more time you put into your work, the better its outcome, but more time means higher costs. The technology has arrived, with talented people everywhere that have access to these great audio and video tools. It's just that old nemesis Time, and how much of it publishers and producers are willing to buy for their production team."

Hoban also has some thoughts on the interplay between the arts and access. "Digital technology has brought us to the verge of disaster—or, quite possibly, a new renaissance. Illegal downloading has crushed the recording business as we know it. The worldwide financial crisis has forced governments to cut back funding for the arts and libraries. However, people are reading, watching videos, and listening to music and audiobooks more than at any time in human history. If we are not careful, we will run out of quality content to listen to and view. Technology has given us the tools to stream content in high quality, high resolution, so let's hope that we, as a society, respect the creators. There will always be those who support artists and want to purchase their favorite works, whether they be books, audiobooks, songs, or movies. However, we also should provide access for the casual listener, the poor, and the curious. The best way to do that is through streaming media, all content available to all at all times. It should be available for free in libraries. It should stream into our homes and onto our personal devices. We have the technology to track downloads and pay a small fee to the creators. Someday, full band-width quality will be available everywhere, and in an instant. It's up to society to provide the framework to administer proper and just remuneration to the content providers. It will happen. Or we'll all be doomed to watch reruns and listen to old, long-dead artists."[2]

AUDIOBOOK AS APP: TRANSMEDIA BLURS THE LINE

As literature moves onto digital devices, the lines blur between book, audio, and image, creating what MIT media studies professor Henry Jenkins has dubbed "transmedia storytelling."[3] Michel Kripalani, founder of Oceanhouse Media, combines words, voice, and animation in book apps that appeal to a wide age range, from toddlers to adults. I spoke with Kripalani in 2011, soon after his company had crossed the one million mark in paid app downloads in Apple's iTunes Store, just two years after the company's start. When asked how his background in the computer and game design fields influenced the development of picture book–based apps, Kripalani replies, "When creating interactive books for children, we are using game engine technology under the hood. We're not just scanning the book's pages and displaying them, we're combining graphics and text, enabling highlighting words and tappable pictures as interactive elements combined to re-create the page. The synergy of these elements and the animations that we use to display them are more akin to a video game than anything else. The experience we have in building games gives us the ability to create a modern architecture that works well for digital interactive children's books."

Kripalani compares the audiobook readalong experience, a physical book–plus–audio recording, with Oceanhouse Media's apps for children: "In a readalong, the child is listening to the book in an engaging and interesting, yet more passive, way. With the apps that we're producing, we are teaching interactive literacy to children. There's a very important, direct connection between what's being spoken and what's being viewed. The tie-in between the graphics, the text, and the audio is critical. The voice-over actor has to speak at a slow, appropriate pace, and the words must highlight perfectly in sync with the narration. This way, as the child is listening to the words, they see those exact words highlighted on the screen. Additionally, we support all of this with picture word association features which allow the child to tap on any picture and see the word enlarged as it is spoken."

Kripalani predicts that the growing convergence of media for young readers will have a great impact on the audiobook publishing business. "I think that media that once stood alone are now being combined into a transmedia experience. Books transforming into interactive apps is an example of that, as are film and TV becoming streaming or app based experiences. When apps combine all of this together, without a doubt there is a full, multimedia experience that will benefit young readers. . . . Audiobook elements are going to be looked at as just one piece of the puzzle. When we developed our *The Cat in the Hat* app, we began with the source material that Dr. Seuss created: the illustrations and the text. The voiceover piece is another element on top, as are the interactive features. The audiobook piece is a very significant component, but it's just one piece of the overall puzzle."

Kripalani notes one significant difference between app-based and traditional publishing: "The dynamic is completely different from the complexities of 'old school' publishing. We are not concerned with printing books in China, shipping them across oceans, inventorying them, dealing with wholesale and direct sales channels, selling through large chain or small bookstores. We have a different channel for selling. We build the app, we package it up, and we provide it to Apple, Google, or any other app marketer that appears on the scene. That's it. From there, the app store does worldwide distribution for us."

As he envisions how libraries can provide app-based books or other new media to readers, Kripalani muses, "We've thought about it, and we'd love to see that happen in the future—hopefully by the time this book is published. I've had conversations with librarians and honestly it's a problem for Apple or other app distribution platforms to solve. It's not something that we app developers can solve. Right now, if Apple wants to create the ability to have multiple users on an iPad or create a loaning system for apps, then we think it would be fantastic for libraries to provide apps. However, at this moment in time, until a few core problems are solved, it's not something that we can do."[4]

Audiobooks have survived many transformations in technology, but the path to excellence remains the same: wonderful stories read by talented narrators, carefully crafted by a first-rate production team. No matter the equipment, human expertise remains the primary factor in giving voice to great literature. In the fast-moving world of digital formats, new methods of audiobook recording and distribution have undoubtedly developed since these words were written. Whether on long-playing LP records or downloaded as book apps, audiobooks transcend the format's container, offering content through the timeless gold standard of the oral tradition.

So the next time you encounter a soul-stirring audiobook, remember to include the entire production team in your applause, from narrator and director to researcher and sound engineer. Even though their names may not be on the tip of your tongue, their talents are ringing in your ears.

NOTES

1. Laura Colebank, in discussion with the author, August 20, 2010.
2. Todd Hobin, in discussion with the author, February 2, 2011.
3. Henry Jenkins, "Transmedia Storytelling," *Technology Review,* January 15, 2003, www.technologyreview.com/biomedicine/13052.
4. Michel Kripalani, in discussion with the author, January 17, 2011.

5 Developing and Maintaining an Audiobook Collection

TODAY'S READER TURNS TO a variety of media to experience stories, toggling between an audiobook in the car, an e-book on the iPad, and a paperback book at home, while the story remains the same—and challenges our long-standing definition of the term *reading*. As families, classrooms, and libraries consider expanding their collections of literature in the twenty-first century, evolving formats provide challenges to developing and maintaining the collection.

TRACKING DOWN TITLES

The quickly changing world of publishing can paralyze selectors hesitant to purchase a possibly short-lived format. As audiobooks shift from physical to digital releases, questions about digital rights management and downloading protocols raise concerns about material ownership versus rental of content. Availability of both broadband for downloading and the physical players necessary for listening to digital content provoke unease about equity of user access. End result? Libraries need to build their audio collections on a just-enough-for-just-right-now basis, focusing on a variety of currently available formats that address the diverse needs of the age and economics of the listener, and allocating limited funding to patron-driven selections.

The notion of education versus entertainment may not be the first thought in selecting an audiobook, but a growing range of titles offers a huge selection, from informational to escapist. Some audiobook publishers have complete courses, developed and recorded by professors with supplemental texts and online exams, such as Recorded Books' Modern Scholar line of products. Other large publishers have expanded their audiobook choices, from offering blockbuster-fiction best sellers to releasing simultaneous audio and print versions of indie favorites and scholarly nonfiction. Quality nonfiction for youth, which often contains essential visuals, may have an additional disk in the physical audiobook edition that includes computer-readable images, or it may combine text, image, and narration in a streaming digital product. Biographies and memoirs are a fast-growing segment of the audiobook market, with the added benefit of an author voicing her own life story. There are even small niche publishers that create audios for a unique clientele, such as Knitting Out Loud. Digital downloads can offer a hybrid product that contains images and professionally narrated audio synced to text. Auditory learners, once frustrated by the nearly nonexistent number of nonfiction audiobooks, now have a multitude of categories to provide enlightenment and education.

When creating a balanced collection, selectors need to consider not only the format and genre of audiobooks but also the range of production and narration methods. Audiobooks are not a one-style-fits-all format. Some listeners gain meaning from evocative audio effects and underlying music. Others are distracted when added music and other sounds compete for attention and prefer only the narrated text. Some listen best when an audio is produced with a full cast of readers portraying the characters. Others have a favorite narrator and will listen to anything read by that actor in his natural voice. Many publishers provide added content such as author interviews. Some publishers specialize in audio recordings of live stage or radio productions. In addition, selectors should provide audios with a variety of playing times, from titles with very short segments, for example short stories or vignettes, to epic-length titles that may span over twenty hours, focusing on the student-friendly sweet spot of three- to five-hour titles. Providing a broad spectrum of audiobook styles allows listeners to find a title that fits their particular mood or personal listening preference.

To provide a diverse collection of audiobooks, selectors must track down titles from a large number of publishers. Consumers, as well as schools and libraries, often turn to large online vendors such as Amazon, Barnes & Noble, or Audible.com to see if a title is available in audio format. However, this will not give a clear picture of the entire range of audio editions produced. Hunting down a book's audio edition can be frustrating. Some audiobook titles are published as both retail and library editions—often by two different companies, with two different narrators, and as abridged and unabridged versions. Just one of those possibilities may be available from a particular online vendor—or none at all. Many titles are released as digital-only products, with no physical edition. Some audio publishers have both a public library division and a school division. Some formats, such as the Playaway version of a publisher's title, may be available through one vendor for the school market, another for the public library market, and directly from the manufacturer's website for consumers. Noncommercial recordings produced for the blind or those who are print disabled usually cannot be found through any commercial vendor.

A simple solution to edition and format overload is to also search the free WorldCat website (www.worldcat.org) , the world's largest catalog of library materials, compiled by OCLC, the Online Computer Library Center. There, you can search for the desired title, narrowing the parameters to *Audiobook, CD,* or *eAudiobook.* The results show the range of formats and editions held in libraries around the world, including international editions and foreign language audio versions, as well as audiobooks available through Recordings for the Blind and Dyslexic. You can then search a commercial source, a school or library wholesale vendor, or the audiobook publisher for a particular edition. Schools and libraries may choose to purchase and repackage a lower-priced retail consumer physical edition, while many institutions choose to purchase directly from the title's publisher to take advantage of sturdy library packaging and lifetime free replacement of physical media. The *AudioFile* website (www.audiofilemagazine .com) has an excellent Audiobook Reference Guide that includes a detailed listing of publishers large and small, with web links and contact information. If a certain audiobook or desired format is currently out of print, there's a possibility that the publisher may have a small number of the title available in stock if you contact them directly.

SELECTION AND PURCHASING

The key to building a quality collection is to evaluate the audiobook production, not solely that of the title's authorial content but of the unique characteristics of the audio format. There's no shortcut here; selectors must put in the time beneath the headphones to develop benchmarks in the spectrum of excellence in audiobook production.

An outstanding resource for those selecting audiobooks for youth is *Listening to Learn: Audiobooks Supporting Literacy* (ALA Editions 2011) by Sharon Grover and Lizette D. Hannegan, both former chairs of the Odyssey Award for Excellence in Audiobook Production Committee, which contains a thorough look at audio methods and titles that support core curriculum educational standards and literacy development. Grover collaborated with ALA's Ethnic and Multicultural Information Exchange Round Table to create the "Read around the World with Your Ears," publications for both kids and teens, providing selectors with audiobook titles that provide an authentic cultural listing experience.[1] Another prime audiobook resource is Joyce Saricks, recognized by ALA's Reference and User Services Division for her work in adult readers' advisory.[2] Saricks often includes ruminations on all things audiobook, applicable to any age listener, in her "At Leisure" column in *Booklist* magazine. She educates selectors on the qualities of an outstanding audiobook review in "Writing Audiobook Reviews," the chapter she authored in Brad Hooper's *Writing Reviews for Readers' Advisory* (ALA Editions 2010). Her book *Read On . . . Audiobooks: Reading Lists for Every Taste* (Libraries Unlimited 2011) lists over three hundred audiobooks for adults, many with teen appeal, categorized into sixty themes.

In *The Readers' Advisory Handbook* (ALA Editions 2010), edited by Jessica E. Moyer and Kaite Mediatore Stover, there are two chapters of interest to those evaluating audiobooks: "How to Listen to a Book in Thirty Minutes," by Stover, and "Reviewing Audiobooks," by *Booklist* media editor Sue-Ellen Beauregard. Other resources to facilitate audiobook evaluation and selection can be found in appendix B of this book, "Recommended Reading."

In times of tight budgets, selectors must balance audiobook purchases with literature in other media formats. For those in public libraries, the audiobook collection might be part of the audiovisual department budget or purchased and circulated by the respective adult/youth/teen/nonfiction departments. In schools, audiobooks may be housed in the library media center or a classroom collection, located in the reading department bookroom, or be part of intervention services collections. No matter where the collection is housed, savvy cash-strapped selectors partner with other entities for additional audiobook funding. For example, a public library's youth services department may lobby the audiovisual department to purchase a separate audiobook collection of titles commonly found on school summer reading lists to be housed in the Teen area. School librarians can explore alternate funding sources for an audiobook collection through local and federal funds targeted for special education, English language learners, or students with disabilities. Support groups such as the Friends of the Library or parent-teacher associations could provide a core audio collection to promote a local "One Book" initiative, to enable a large-print book plus audio collection, to support a parent-child audiobook club, or to purchase audio versions of required school summer reading requirements. Local education foundation organizations may have grants to create similar projects or to jump-start a collection of audiobooks in a format currently not available, such as easy-to-use, preloaded Playaway units for special needs patrons or the very young. National chains such as Dollar General, Walmart, or Target have grant opportunities for organizations providing educational resources to the community. For further library grant ideas, visit the Library Grants blog (www.librarygrants.blogspot.com) or search the ALA website (www.ala.org) and search on *grants*, *awards*, or *fellowships*.

In this book, you'll find tips in chapter 6, "Listening with a Critical Ear," which notes the factors especially important for those choosing titles for children and young adults, with examples of exemplary productions. Chapter 2, "What Is an Audiobook? Why Listen?" supplies a rationale to justify the addition of audios for youth in the library collection, while the glossary found in appendix A will provide the specialized lingo to inform your audiobook discussions. Reading audiobook reviews in professional journals—such as the resources listed in chapter 7, "Audiobook Awards and Recognition"—will build a foundation of knowledge. ALA provides a continually updated core collection through the yearly youth audiobook award and selection lists found in chapter 7. Plus, you can find expert audiobook advice in a variety of American Library Association blogs, journal articles, and publications by searching on *audiobook* in the ALA Store (www.alastore.ala.org) or BooklistOnline (www.booklistonline.com).

MEETING USER NEEDS

As you build your collection, consult with local groups for a needs assessment that targets the audiobook format. An audiobook survey or suggested purchase request, either at the library circulation desk or on the website, serves to gather user input on formats, popular titles, or other topics. Local language arts, special education, and ELL teachers will provide lists of core titles to match curriculum needs. Children and adults who attend story time or other library programming can form a focus group to advise on usability of digital and physical formats, as well as desired purchases, for both the typical and special needs populations. Teen advisory groups or book club members will happily peruse audiobook catalogs to supply patron-requested wish lists. School and public librarians may partner to inform one another about user needs and collaborate on solutions, such as school librarians encouraging public library audiobook downloads and facilitating public library card applications in the school setting. Digital download providers can enable automatic patron-driven acquisition of titles and supply statistics on high-demand titles, which can be used to lobby consortia members to increase purchase of youth audiobooks. Consulting with other community organizations—such as preschools, city planning committees, and literacy programs—will provide additional information on cultural groups, local demographics, and access to broadband technology, allowing selectors to carefully choose an audio collection that matches users' needs.

As libraries move toward digital-only audiobooks, decisions about changing technologies and physical formats must be made. Are there still users who want titles on cassette or other discontinued media? Have an information sheet that lists remaining titles—and solicit donations to supplement the remaining collection. Is it cost effective to purchase Playaways or library editions of physical audiobooks, or will cheaper consumer editions of titles on CD serve until the transition to digital is made? Is it worthwhile to maintain a separate collection of physical titles once an institution switches primarily to downloads? Decide whether to interfile remaining physical audiobooks with print editions or to continue separate shelving. Want to keep physical audios and preloaded units but find that users no longer have the required players or battery sizes? Investigate purchasing circulating players and rechargeable batteries. These investigations and interactions with users will also help determine the nitty-gritty of access and circulation. Are patrons hampered by fines, fees, circulation loan periods, and renewal limits? Survey all age groups and format users to determine each segment's opinion. Are users confused by the library's online catalog or digital download web page? Seek advice from user groups who are solely digital download patrons and never enter the library.

Keeping up with changing trends in digital technology and literacy development will also help guide planning for the future needs of patrons. Those selecting materials will have a host of blogs and resources in their personal learning network, but be sure to include the following. For insightful overviews on the changing landscape of technology and literacy for both children and adults, explore the trend data collected by the Pew Research Center's Internet & American Life Project (www.pewinternet.org). The Cooney Center (www.joanganzcooneycenter.org), founded by Sesame Street creator Joan Ganz Cooney, focuses on how digital media technologies advance children's literacy and learning. The International Reading Association (www.reading.org) offers information on the changing landscape of literacy development. Continuous assessment of user needs is crucial during fast-changing technological times and will allow you to balance your collection to meet shifting expectations.

MARKETING AND PROMOTING

Promoting audiobooks to users can be as straightforward as a face-to-face recommendation, offering the right book in the right format at the right time. Or an eye-catching display in a community gathering place may entice those who never set foot in the library to download their first audiobook title. Whether personal or passive, marketing the audiobook collection is essential for increasing patron usage.

Looking to encourage audiobook use by kids and teens? Hook parents and teachers first, and let these trusted adults provide word-of-mouth audiobook recommendations. Set up displays of family-friendly audiobooks for on-the-go listening before the next holiday break or on parent-teacher open house night, as well as posting a recommendation list on the library website. Create displays or handouts that give suggestions of audios that fit listening time blocks, from short trips around town up to audiobooks long enough for cross-country trips. Offer to be a virtual shopper, willing to match both a child's interests and family vacation travel time, and package a collection of audiobooks from the school library for over-the-summer checkout. Highlight your audiobook collection during toddler time and in parent e-mail newsletters, along with research data explaining how listening to literature benefits literacy.

Convert a teacher with a long commute by slipping a surefire YA audiobook into her work mailbox, and gain an adult ready to share favorites with students. Offer to speak to interested educators, booktalking the audio collection and distributing handouts from audiobook publishers that detail educational benefits (see appendix B, "Recommended Reading"). Target intervention specialists who work with youth with identified special needs and share how the audiobook collection specifically benefits groups from toddlers with developmental disabilities to gifted and talented high school students. Step outside the library to promote summertime family listening at the local pool, with posters that promote online library card application and digital downloads. Adult coaches and youth advisors are ideal partners who welcome suggestions of audiobooks that will allow students to keep up with required reading by listening on the bus or while waiting for club events, or maybe even during practice sessions. Adults who take advantage of these audiobook promotions will encourage kids to listen, and might become an eager audiobook patrons themselves.

Today's young people are naturals in a transmedia world where stories and information take many formats. Introducing these digital natives to literature as audiobooks can be as easy as maintaining a format-neutral policy when referring to reading. When giving readers' advisory recommendations or creating summer reading lists, be sure to note all available formats, both physical and digital. Include audiobooks in displays and book talks, getting creative when a title is only available in a digital format—perhaps include a short audio clip or link, and show a digital dummy, a color printout of the book cover inserted in a salvaged audiobook CD case or iPod mock up. Incorporate listening minutes in summer reading club requirements and lobby for audiobooks fulfilling reading assignments by teachers. Include audiobooks in curriculum pathfinders and classroom collections, and promote audiobooks on the library website and social media outlets, friending audiobook publishers who may offer giveaways or contests. Piggyback with promotions from the Audio Publishers Association (www.audiopub.org) or the Audiobook Community Facebook group (www.facebook.com/audiobookcommunity), such as the SYNC summertime promo of free audiobook downloads for teens or YouTube audiobook video trailer contests.

Give kids a chance to try out audiobooks by providing listening stations in youth and teen areas and by creating a student listening club or a parent-child audiobook group. Libraries that have large physical collections of audiobooks will want to include a circulating collection of inexpensive players to increase use. Kids may have only digital players and may ask for advice on how to rip an audiobook on CD or flash drive to load onto their personal MP3 player or cell phone. Remind them about the importance of following copyright law and to treat this transfer exactly like a checked-out physical item, deleting and destroying the title immediately after listening in order to "check it in," and to never share the file. Tie audiobooks to youth services programming, Teen Read Week, or Tech Week by hosting a gadget petting zoo, demonstrating how to download audiobooks and e-books onto a variety of digital devices; offer to host similar events off-site for local organizations such as Scouts or after-school programs. Multitasking teens will appreciate displays of audiobooks in collaboration with craft programs on knitting or beadwork, or alongside workout DVDs. Include diverse audiobook styles in promotions—single-voice, full cast, nonfiction—as well as a range of playing times to offer variety once a young listener becomes an audiobook connoisseur. Get audio-savvy youth volunteers into the audio promotion act, with a multigenerational program where teens travel to the local senior citizen center and teach how to download audiobooks and e-books onto e-readers, and demo Playaways paired with large print books to senior groups. Feature these teens in how-to videos demonstrating digital downloads and recommending favorite titles in audiobook trailers on the library website.

POLICY GUIDES COLLECTION DEVELOPMENT

All the steps involved in developing and maintaining an audiobook collection for school and public libraries or other institutions should be guided by a clear and comprehensive materials selection policy. This policy should describe the objectives in creating the collection; who is responsible for selection; the selection criteria; the procedures in evaluating, purchasing, processing, and circulating the materials; and policy on special areas or collections, such as donations. As with any formal statement, periodic revision should assess the policies for language that must be removed, changed, or added to address changing situations. The fast-changing world of digital publishing has impact on many points of policy. For example, does your policy list fines for overdue audiobooks, when you've switched to a digital-only automatic check-in collection? Libraries have taken steps to change to a more format-agnostic language that allows for new technology in formal statements, using the "Workbook for Selection Policy Writing" found on the American Library Association's website.[3] ALA's Public Library Association and American Association of School Librarians division websites, as well as state library and regional consortia, will have sample policies to use as models. An excellent document to use as an example is "Guidelines for Media Resources in Academic Libraries," drafted July 2011, by a Task Force of the Association of College and Research Libraries.[4] Although geared toward college libraries, the guidelines reflect sound standards for any media collection. It is especially important to be aware of the library's statements on Intellectual Freedom, policies on controversial materials, and guidelines for handling patron requests for reconsidering challenged material. Those selecting materials in the audio format must deliberate the difference between reading text that contains strong language or emotional content and hearing the words spoken aloud. The impact on listeners can be very different when the material's format does not allow skimming over content or mentally bleeping a word. A book automatically added to the print title shelf may require a carefully considered purchasing rationale for the audiobook, one that clearly follows the policies in place and can be defended using the challenged materials reconsideration process. The National Council of Teachers of English (www.ncte.org) and ALA's Office for Intellectual Freedom (www.ala.org/oif/) offer tremendous resources for making informed material selection policies, including the essential "Guidelines for Dealing with Censorship of Nonprint and Multimedia Materials" from NCTE.[5]

SPOTLIGHT REFLECTION

Listening with Open Ears: Audiobooks and Intellectual Freedom *BY DR. TERI S. LESESNE*

AS A LONGTIME ADVOCATE of audiobooks both personally and professionally, I have been heartened to see more attention cast on this format. The Odyssey Award, a joint award of ALSC and YALSA, has done much to put the spotlight on audiobooks. Articles in journals have offered the research base for including audiobooks in classrooms. Sales of audiobooks have grown during a period of time when print book sales are down. All of this is the good news. So, you know what is coming, right? I believe firmly that, as audiobooks make inroads into the schools, they, too, will become the targets of censors. After all, we have seen this same phenomenon with the increased use of trade books. Annual reports from the ALA's Office of Intellectual Freedom note the challenges issued against contemporary titles. Many of the Top Ten Challenged Books are available in audio format, including *The Chocolate War, The Color Purple, To Kill a Mockingbird,* and *Twilight.* Additionally, the Top Banned Classics include audio favorites such as *The Wizard of Oz, Charlotte's Web,* and *Winnie the Pooh.* Take a glance at the Common Sense Media website (www.commonsensemedia .org) and see cautionary notes for 2010 Printz Honor winners *The Monstrumologist* and *Punkzilla,* among others.

What does this mean? I wrote "The Next Battleground: Audiobooks and Censorship," a teacher's guide for Random House, a few years ago (see appendix B, "Recommended Reading"). I think that as the use of audiobooks becomes more prevalent, we will see a commensurate increase in challenges to this format. From my perspective, as someone who works with preservice and in-service librarians, this means we need to become proactive and not wait for the battle to begin. The Office of Intellectual Freedom (OIF) of ALA reports that chief among the reasons for challenges are: sexual content, objectionable language, mention of the occult, and violence. That would make *In the Belly of the Bloodhound, The Absolutely True Diary of a Part-Time Indian,* and *Harry Potter and the Deathly Hallows*—all Odyssey Award Winners or Odyssey Honors—potential targets of censors, to name just a few titles.

If challenges are to come, we need to be prepared in advance. What should we include in a tool kit we might label "Open in case of closed minds"?

> We need to check our collection development policies and make sure they cover audiobooks.
>
> We need to be certain that our Reconsideration of Materials policies cover audiobooks as well.
>
> We need to have rationales for audiobooks that might be used in a classroom/instructional setting. These rationales need to mirror those completed for potentially difficult texts.
>
> We need to read reviews of audiobooks, seeking the best ones available for our students.
>
> Most important, we need to be careful listeners of audiobooks ourselves. My colleagues who were part of the inaugural Odyssey Committee noticed that we were becoming more and more attentive to things in our listening. We called this phenomenon "listening with our Odyssey ears." We all need to develop this skill of listening attentively.

Audiobooks are important whether we are "racing to the top" or "leaving no child behind," or just making a commute more endurable and enjoyable. For some, audiobooks are an important first step on the road to becoming a lifelong reader. For others, they are a tool that permits them to find more time to read. Adding audiobooks—especially those that cause the reader to *think* about the book and leave the story with more questions than answers—is one way we can welcome more readers to the wonderful world of books. Being prepared for the challenges we might face down the road ensures that we continue to grow our audiobook collections, that we continue to reach out to readers of all ages and abilities, and that we stay constantly aware of the key role we play when we open someone's ears to the world of audiobooks.

Teri S. Lesesne is a professor at Sam Houston State University and the author of **Making the Match** *(Stenhouse 2003),* **Naked Reading** *(Stenhouse 2006), and* **Reading Ladders** *(Heinemann 2010).*

NOTES

1. Ethnic & Multicultural Information Exchange Round Table, American Library Association, http://www.ala.org/emiert/.

2. "Joyce Saricks Wins 2011 RUSA Margaret Monroe Award," *RUSABlog* (blog), March 31, 2011, http://rusa.ala.org/blog/2011/03/31/2011 -monroe/.

3. "Workbook for Selection Policy Writing," American Library Association, revised October, 1998, www.ala.org/Template.cfm?Section = dealing& Template = /ContentManagement/ContentDisplay.cfm&ContentID = 11173.

4. "Guidelines for Media Resources in Academic Libraries (Draft)," American Library Association, July 2011, www.ala.org/ala/mgrps/ divs/acrl/standards/media_resources_draf.pdf.

5. "Guidelines for Dealing with Censorship of Nonprint and Multimedia Materials," Standing Committee against Censorship, National Council of Teachers of English, revised October 2004, www.ncte.org/positions/ statements/censorshipofnonprint.

6 Listening with a Critical Ear

WITH A FIRM GROUNDING in audiobook history, supplied with a rational for including literature in audiobook format in literacy development, armed with a clear collection policy and plan for selection and promotion, enlightened on the path of audiobook creation—it's time to focus on the individual qualities that are key to quality productions. Beyond the literary features that are common to discussions about print titles, what special characteristics should be considered when selecting books that have been transformed into audiobooks?

LEARN THE LINGO

Analyzing audiobooks calls for accurate terminology to define the qualities inherent in an aural medium—qualities that are as critical to an exemplary audiobook as literary elements are to the analysis of text. Readers begin using specific vocabulary in the primary classroom when describing literary elements such as character, setting, and plot. Audiobook listeners perceive the aspects that affect the impact of an audiobook, but they may not know the language used by the audiobook professionals. When we discuss audiobooks, we begin with the core—the original book—conversing comfortably about the familiar literary essentials. But when we move beyond the book, into the realm of describing what is heard, we think, "There's got to be a word for this!" During my tenure as chair of ALA's Odyssey Award for Excellence in Audiobook Production committee, I set upon a quest to compile the terms and phrases that producers and directors use as they craft their work. A stellar group of audiobook leaders shared with me the industry idioms that pin down our aural perceptions. The result? An "Audiobook Lexicon" that covers the good (*listener engagement*), the bad (*dry mouth*), and the ugly (*woofing the mic*). Originally printed in *AudioFile,*[1] an updated list of audiobook lingo can be found in appendix A. Include these terms in the classroom, literature discussion groups, and casual conversation with young digital natives who toggle seamlessly between print, audiobook, and e-book in a brave new world of digital transliteracy.

When listening critically to an audiobook, the experience is so much more than the re-creation of the text. The interplay between content and production is a balancing act between two sides of a seesaw. An award-winning print title may be a poorly produced audiobook with lackluster narration, resulting in an audio experience where the production side falls far below the text. A marginal print title may find a quirky interpretation with a gifted narrator that raises the production level and reenvisions the work. A truly touchstone audiobook finds the perfect balance—a faultless interpretation of meaningful content in both soundscape and narration.

NARRATION AS FOUNDATION

What are the qualities of a touchstone audiobook? Narration is the foundation, providing the author's voice directly to the listener, removing our unconscious filtering of the text through our own internal voice. The reading must be authentic and appropriate to the content; the narrator must create voicings that match the time and place of the text, as well as each character's age, culture, and mood. A single performer may choose a variety of styles, from reading in a natural voice to creating individual voicings for characters. Multiple narrators may be used, resulting in discreet segments of a title performed by different readers or in a full-cast interpretation. No matter the style of narration, some elements are critical. The narrator must maintain individual character voicings, accents, or dialects consistently throughout the audiobook; be able to reveal the context of line through inflection and emphasis; and convey the meaning of the text through expression, emotion, and energy. The voice should not sound strained or overplayed, and should be free of stilted, monotonous, or repetitive rhythms. Cultures should be represented by authentic narration and presented without stereotype. The reading should be free of distractions such as mispronounced words or a mismatch of dialogue description ("he murmured") and line reading. Special challenges include place names, foreign terminology, and invented words. Other distractions may result if the reader's mouth sounds become dry, breathy, or juicy, or move off-microphone. Touchstone narration is transparent, staying true to the spirit and content of the text, while forging a direct, personal connection between the listener and the author's words.

An audiobook for young people requires a narrator who gives extra attention to needs of this particular audience when performing, measuring pace and tempo to match the listener's comprehension. The skill of a narrator to translate convoluted and sometimes archaic sentence structure into the comprehensible flow of natural speech, while allowing enough audible white space to digest content, is especially important on audiobook versions of classics often found on required reading lists. For two excellent examples applicable for teen listeners, compare the multivoiced production of *Frankenstein* (2009) from the Naxos Audiobook Young Adult Classic series (which contains an abridged audio recording, plus a CD-ROM containing a study guide and both the abridged and unabridged text) with Tantor Media's 2008 Unabridged Classics *Frankenstein* version, which features *Booklist*'s "Voice of Choice" Simon Vance narrating (and includes both an unabridged audiobook recording and a PDF e-book). Yet this same skill is equally important in titles for the youngest reader, where the simplified sentence structure found in beginning books for emerging readers can—when voiced by a poor narrator—result in a flat, sing-song cadence that sounds condescending to a child. Contrast this with the altogether perfect recording of the *Frog and Toad Audio Collection* (HarperAudio 2004), where author Arnold Lobel charmingly narrates a faultless companion for children combining the audio with the classic text and illustrations, which were awarded both the Newbery and Caldecott honor medals. Whether accomplished or novice, all types of readers find a path to greater fluency and meaning through nuanced inflection and well-paced narration.

Books that feature a first-person point of view often translate beautifully into audio format, but with one important caveat when choosing titles: the narrator must match the age of the protagonist. Children and teen listeners are especially critical when a voice is jarringly dissimilar from the mental audio image of a character. Audio producers sometimes cast young readers, such as 11-year-old Everette Plen in the Alvin Ho series (Listening Library), to authentically voice a character. Other productions depend on adult actors who are expert in communicating a fresh innocence and lightness of voice, such as Jessica Almasy, whose youthful narration can be heard on numerous titles including the Clementine series (Recorded Books); or Nick Podehl, who nails the endearing awkwardness of teen guy-dom, as on *Carter Finally Gets It* (Brilliance Audio 2009). Many young listeners appreciate Full Cast Audio's philosophy of casting age-appropriate actors for their multivoiced productions, becoming fans of the company's repertory group of tween and teen readers. The experience of hearing a youthful narrator's voice engages young listeners and forges an instant connection to the story and characters.

Accents and dialects—vital for providing a young listener with a strong sense of place and culture—pose a challenge for the audiobook narrator, while correctly pronounced words are as important as correctly spelled words in a print title. Books that feature nonnative language terms must provide an accurate foundation for listeners who are hearing foreign words spoken aloud for the first time, while young listeners from a particular region or culture in an audio must perceive their reality portrayed with genuine and careful respect. The listener is invited to a place evoked by the aural environment; such is the case with the mix of Spanish words and Latino accents in the Los Angeles of Willie Colon's authentically voiced *Chato's Kitchen* (Live Oak Media 2003) or the small-town South Carolina heard in Scott Sowers' rural drawl as he reads *The Small Adventure of Popeye and Elvis* (Recorded Books 2009). Audiobook producers should seek narrators who can accurately speak the languages in a title, with special care to reflect the cultures and regions involved. British actor Allan Corduner's brilliant reading of *The Book Thief* (Listening Library 2006) owes much to his ability to correctly speak German, which he learned from his mother, who escaped Nazi Germany. When Scholastic Audio recorded *Words in the Dust* (2012), actress Ariana Delawari, whose parents live in Kabul, was cast after an extensive search for a reader who could provide both an accurate Afghanistan accent and an appropriately youthful voice to match that of the 13-year-old protagonist. In *The Power of One* (Bolinda Audio 2007), the South African culture of the 1930s and 1940s is brilliantly portrayed by Australian stage actor Humphrey Bower as he shifts from a Boer accent to Afrikaans, Zulu, or European, demonstrating that authenticity need not be native-born. Author Harper Lee personally approved the selection of Sissy Spacek, who voiced the fiftieth anniversary audio edition of *To Kill a Mockingbird* (Caedmon 2006) in her trademark Southern lilt. Each of these titles honors the literary work by providing a voice that is true to the intent of the author, adding color and clarity to illuminate meaning.

Master narrators take an author's book and craft performances that transcend the printed page, creating a benchmark audio. A discussion of audiobook narrators would be incomplete without honoring Jim Dale, who has been awarded the Member of the Order of the British Empire by Queen Elizabeth II for his work promoting English children's literature and appears in the Guinness World Records for Most Character Voices in an Audiobook (146!) for his role as the American voice of the Harry Potter series—but any book he performs will be forever transformed.[2] The best narrators are actors who specialize in audiobook performance, but some celebrities are surprisingly fine behind the microphone, with Meryl Streep and Stanley Tucci's reading of *The One and Only Shrek! and 8 Other Stories* (Macmillan Young Listeners 2007) one of the best. Authors who are consummate narrators are few and far between, but two who deserve special recognition are Neil Gaiman and Jack Gantos—both have recorded many of their own books brilliantly. The entire roster of performers who appear on Odyssey Award–winning and Odyssey Honor audiobook titles are must-listen voices, each crafting an unforgettable experience. Selectors should make special note of these fine actors who have a special ability to connect with young people: Gerard Doyle, Judith Ivey, Jenna Lamia, Johnny Heller, Robin Miles, Will Patton, Cassandra Morris, and Simon Prebble. Each will supply listeners with immeasurable listening enjoyment and provide selectors with the benchmarks of narrator excellence.

PRODUCTION QUALITY CONTROL

Production factors work in tandem with the narration to create a soundscape that evokes a total emotional engagement with the audio experience. Sloppy direction and editing may result in segments with uneven pacing, missing or repeated text, sibilant or plosive microphone pickups, a "hot" quality that is too loud or intense, obvious dubbing of retakes, or abrupt or lengthy breaks between lines or chapters. Poorly produced sessions may contain segments recorded at noticeably different times, where the listener can perceive the narrator's loss of energy, rather than quality editing where segments are acoustically identical and demonstrate the narrator's vocal stamina. Quality productions have a clean, crisp sound that allows for periods of silence and a range of dynamics without affecting volume levels, creating a seamless narrative that gives the impression of a single take.

Packaging, formatting, and describing the audiobook are also important points in evaluating audiobooks. Sloppy processing has resulted in packaging where the title is incorrect, the author and narrator's names misspelled, the gender of the characters mistaken, and other egregious errors. Selectors should monitor accuracy in the final product that impacts listener selection and enjoyment. Audio announcement of CD number, the message that announces the beginning or end of a side or segment and other navigation information, called *side tags*, serve to guide listeners through the production. Formatting the audio to fit a CD or other format should provide manageable chapters and logical splits between segments of the production, leaving no unconnected widow or orphan sentence fragments or paragraph breaks. An audiobook may be abridged or unabridged, have special or bonus features such as author interviews, may or may not contain collateral material from the print title such as time lines and back matter, or have enhanced digital content such as images. All these features should be noted in the library catalog and in any descriptive materials. Audiobook listeners depend on descriptive notes that contain accurate run times of the total production while providing both author and narrator names, as well as other material such as original cover art and recommended ages.

ALIVE WITH THE SOUND OF MUSIC

Suitable musical segments, or *tags*, may serve to set the scene at the beginning, or *intro*, of the audiobook, giving a hint of location or historical era. Music may be present at the beginning of individual CDs or segments, may appear a subtle bed under the narration, or may delineate changes of time period or setting. Musical tags may also cue the last part of a segment or side of a CD, or of the audiobook production, through an *outro* (a selection that marks the end of the portion). Occasionally, an original musical soundbed is composed to orchestrate the entire audiobook. If sound effects are used, they serve to enhance the soundscape by expanding the text's meaning, not duplicating narration; that is, the sentence "He knocked" does not need to be followed by a sound of a knock at the door. Music and sound effect should serve to support—never supplant—the narrator's voice, enriching the production in a way that subtly adds meaning to the author's message.

Young listeners can benefit greatly by the context created by music and sound effects. The combination allows a subliminal recognition of setting, mood, culture, and time period. Live Oak Media specializes in crafting evocative soundscapes that integrate musical compositions and subtle environmental sounds, such as in *Jazz* (2007) and *Here in Harlem* (2011), where the poetry of Walter Dean Myers is enhanced with musical selections that convey the shifting time periods. Full Cast Audio productions are frequently excellent examples of a rich aural atmosphere that mixes original musical soundtracks and cinematic sound effects to provide a backdrop for multivoiced performances, such as in the Airborn series. Hachette Audio's production of *Nelson Mandela's Favorite African Folktales* (2009) combines performances by a pantheon of celebrity narrators with an original musical score by South African musical legends Johnny Clegg and Vusi Mahlasela to ground the tales in cultural authenticity. *The Revenge of the Whale* (Audio Bookshelf 2005) contains hauntingly sung, authentic sea shanties, transporting listeners into this true story of shipwrecked horror. Scholastic Audio's hilarious production of *Beauty Queens* (2011) features terrific narration by author-narrator Libba Bray and quirky sound effects and distortions to indicate footnotes and authorial asides. Deborah Wiles's novel *Countdown* (Listening Library 2011) contains images and scrapbook-like graphic snippets that are superbly translated into an audible historical setting in the audio production. Each of these examples keeps the text as the primary focus while transforming the work with thoughtful interpretations of literary context into sound.

RIGORS OF READALONG AUDIOBOOKS AND APPS

Readalongs must accurately convey the meaning of both the text and the illustrations through the audiobook soundscape, and avoid mismatches between the words, pictures, and sound effects. The very young may experience the production as a book-plus-audio readalong package or in a digital environment that includes pictures, narrated text, music, and sound effects. The light-hearted mood of *Click Clack Moo: Cows That Type* (Weston Woods, 2001) is conveyed through sound effects that provide the barnyard setting and provide the contextual clack of an actual typewriter, as narrator (and country music artist) Randy Travis's original music accompanies his down-home drawl, all perfectly paced to allow little ones new to the conventions of text to follow the words supported by an accurate reading, while leaving plenty of time for decoding the illustrations and leisurely page turns. The craft of translating a thirty-two-page book with a limited number of words into an audiobook might seem a simple task when compared to recording a five-hundred-page epic novel. Yet the flawless production of a readalong is a rare occasion. It's an exacting task to compose audible effects that enhance picture content, convey the concept of punctuation and sense of tracking text, set a story in culture and historical accuracy through music, and orchestrate all these to reflect the author's mood, tone, and meaning. A small error or imperfection in a readalong will be spotted by eagle-eyed (and -eared!) toddlers, who revisit a book-plus-audio favorite again and again, while teen listeners enthralled by an audio performance may never know if the narrator has missed a word or inaccurately spoken a line of text. When selecting audiobooks, the pursuit for the absolutely flawless production is not the goal; instead, it is a quest for an immersive literary experience that touches the soul.

The advent of book apps that combine text, narration, music, sound effects, and animation owe much to the readalong audiobook experience. It is up to evaluators to determine whether the app honors the original content with enhancements to the author's work that support literacy, rather than turning the book into a character-branded video game. A children's picture book app that will provide grounding in the literary experience puts the emphasis on pictures and book, supplying sound and animation, and integrating all into engaging storytelling. An app should feature a skilled human reader who effectively communicates authentic characterization and emotion, and whose speech may be carefully synced to highlight individual words. Products that supply text-to-speech—words that are translated from text and "spoken" by a computerized program— are riddled with inappropriate pronunciations, mismatched emphasis, and awkward phrasing—all detrimental to fluency. When evaluating an app, consider: Do tappable elements and animations interfere with the artwork, text, and narration, or override the ability of a child to stay in control of the story's progress? Does the flow of the product honor the conventions of text, such as left-to-right, top-to-bottom tracking across the page, and the integrity of the original book's layout? As the lines blur between media, stick to the basics and apply common standards of excellence applied across changing formats as we enter a world of transliteracy.

The evaluation of an audiobook must start with the audio and lead to the meaning of the work. Each facet of the audio production must reach a level of excellence where the wall of performance is removed and the listener enters the author's creation. A truly touchstone audiobook eliminates the awareness of the format and allows the listener to fall into a direct sensory experience of story. This phenomenon restores the earliest form of literature, the oral tradition, and brings the audiobook listener back into the virtual warmth of the storyteller's circle.

SPOTLIGHT REFLECTION

Don't Mess with the Story *BY JOYCE G. SARICKS*

I LOVE STORY—IN PRINT, on the small and big screens, and in audio. I will listen to almost anything that provides me with that pleasure, from literary fiction and nonfiction to every type of genre. Narrators of audiobooks make it happen for me. Not only do I listen to more books than I read these days, but I also listen to a much wider range of titles than I'm willing to sit and read. While I have my favorite narrators and ones that

I generally avoid, I would argue that narrators overall are far superior to those of twenty years ago. They entice me into books I don't expect to appreciate, and they enhance my pleasure in the works of authors I love.

That said, there are mistakes that make me downright cranky. First and foremost is pronunciation. I have been known to grind my teeth and practically throw my iPod against the wall upon hearing Chicago's Devon Avenue pronounced like the English county Devon. (Hello, it should sound like de-VON.) That they are spelled the same is no excuse. Or Lisle, Ilinois, pronounced as if it were in France, rather than like "Lyle Lovett." Is it too much to ask that pronunciations should be accurate for the locale? If the narrator doesn't know that when the Arkansas River runs through Kansas, it's pronounced Ar-KANsas, he should. These errors throw us listeners out of the story and frankly make the narration suspect. If the narrator cannot get a town or river right, who's to say she isn't massacring the author's name as well?

Mistakes in foreign pronunciations also make me crazy. I only know German, and I hear so many errors with German words and proper names that I fear the problems are universal. Some narrators are scrupulous about searching out correct pronunciations and language cadences. I wish others were less careless—or that audiobook producers did a better job of checking and correcting these errors.

Having said all this, it might be surprising to hear that I'm not so fussy about accents. For some listeners accents are vital to the success of the production. That's not true for me. Certainly, I like to be able to tell who is speaking among the characters from changes in pitch and tone. If the narrator employs an accent, foreign or regional, I expect it to be accurate and consistently applied, but I often don't notice its presence or absence unless it doesn't sound right or intrudes on the storytelling. Sometimes I suspect narrators don't read the book carefully before hand. I recently listened to a book that included a young, supposedly American man, who midway through the book was identified as a New Zealander who had gone to college in the United States. Oops. He had too big a role to allow the narrator to go back and give him the proper accent. A small gaffe, perhaps, but a telling one.

For me, the audiobook experience is more than accents and character portrayal. More than any other element, tone sets the stage for the storytelling. Narrators need to sound as if they understand and appreciate the story and to reflect this change through pace, character portrayal, and tone. If they're not interested in what they're reading, I won't be either. I gave up on Dostoyevsky years ago after listening to a particularly flat reading of *Crime and Punishment*. I don't expect over-the-top portrayals—unless the work calls for that—but I expect performances that make the most of the material, that leave me satisfied but still hungry for more. Narrators should reflect the author's intention and enhance the story, not distract from it. I want to hear the fear, the passion, the humor assigned by the author reflected in the reader's voice. More than anything else, emotion pulls me into the story and involves me. Without that, it's just a pile of words.

Joyce G. Saricks is the author of **Read On . . .** *Audiobooks (**Libraries Unlimited 2011**).*

NOTES

1. Mary Burkey, "Talking the Talk: An Audiobook Lexicon," *AudioFile*, October/November 2007, www.audiofilemagazine.com/features/fea1007.html.

2. "Harry Potter Narrator Jim Dale Talks with GWR," Guinness World Records, posted 2009, accessed May 24, 2012, http://community .guinnessworldrecords.com/_Harry-Potter-narrator-Jim-Dale-talks-with -GWR/video/713225/7691.html.

7 Audiobook Awards and Recognition

AS AUDIOBOOKS HAVE ENTERED the literary landscape and evaluators of spoken word productions have developed specific standards for excellence, recognition and awards shine a spotlight on the best available titles. From lists that aid professional librarians to industry awards bestowed by recording professionals, each recognition is based on different criteria and offers noteworthy titles for audiobook listeners. Use these lists as an annual update for your core collection, providing you and your patrons with the best in sound literature.

AUDIOBOOKS AND THE AMERICAN LIBRARY ASSOCIATION

The American Library Services for Children division of the American Library Association (ALSC) names selected titles as Notable Children's Recordings (NCR) each January, providing librarians, educators, and parents with an annotated list of recorded music, storytelling and audiobooks for children from birth through age 14. (This list was originally compiled by the Recordings Evaluation Committee of the Children's Services Division, and first appeared as the Notable Children's Recordings and Retrospective Recordings List in the Winter 1977 issue of *Top of the News,* the journal of the Children's Services Division, in the same year that the Children's Services Division changed its name to ALSC.) Over time the respective percentage of music and spoken word publications recognized on the NCR list has shifted, with the early years featuring a larger proportion of music and later years more spoken word, as well as variations in the number of titles produced for younger and older children. It's fascinating to look at the archive of all the NCR lists on the ALSC website, tracking the growing inclusion of intermediate and young adult materials, the increasing length of audiobooks, the appearance of nonfiction titles, and the shift in physical format. The NCR list, now published each January immediately following the ALA Midwinter Meeting, provides a can't-miss shopping list for audiobook selectors. Plus, the current committee's discussion titles, viewable on the ALSC site prior to the Midwinter Meeting, expands the consideration list even further. More important, the NCR criteria document serves as a ready reference for audiobook evaluation, honed by committee use and revision over the years.[1]

In 1991, YALSA, the American Library Association's Young Adult Library Services Association division, initiated its recognition of spoken word recordings for listeners ages 12 through 18, the Selected List of Audio Books for Young Adults, as a function of the Media Selection and Usage Committee of YALSA. In 2009 the list was renamed Amazing Audiobooks for Young Adults.[2] As with NCR, the archived selection lists on the ALA website reflect the changes and developments in YA audiobook production over the years, with an interesting twist: adult titles of interest to teens may be included in the suggested titles. Plus, there are slight differences in the selection criteria between NCR and Amazing Audiobooks that point out subtle differences that a selector might appraise when choosing titles for young adults or younger children; for example, the YALSA list skews to titles that have "teen appeal."[3] The archived lists of both committees testify to the diligence of members to seek out excellent spoken word recordings from all sources, including selections from English-language producers such as British companies Naxos Audio and AudioGo (formerly BBC Audiobooks) and Australian audiobook publisher Bolinda, as well as audiobooks from small independent producers. As the age categories of NCR and Amazing Audiobooks overlap, some titles may appear on both lists. In addition, a title may be recognized by NCR in one year but by Amazing Audiobooks the next; this is because the YALSA list may include titles released within the previous twenty-four months, while NCR limits eligibility to twelve months. Both sets of criteria make for great tools, not only for those purchasing audiobooks, but for listeners of all ages to become savvy critics.

In August 2005, YALSA President Pam Spencer Holley, along with ALSC President Ellen Fader, spearheaded a unique collaboration between ALA divisions with the creation of a task force to investigate an award recognizing excellence in audiobook production for children and young adults. The Odyssey Award for Excellence in Audiobook Production was approved by the ALA Board in June 2006, marking the first time ALA divisions had jointly developed and administered a literary award. The award, sponsored by *Booklist* magazine, recognizes a single winner for the highest achievement in audiobook production for children and/or young adults (up to and including age 18), along with possible honor titles.[4]

The first Odyssey Award committee convened in January 2007, announcing the first Odyssey winner—Live Oak Media for *Jazz*, written by Walter Dean Myers and illustrated by Christopher Myers—at the Youth Media Awards press conference in January 2008. After receiving the Odyssey award, Arnie Cardillo, the producer of *Jazz,* reflected on the impact of the American Library Association's audiobook evaluation committees in an interview for *Booklist* magazine:

> I can't speak for all producers, but the listening criteria and the dedication to the selection process have made me a better producer. The fact that committees are listening closely has made me listen more closely as well, to pay attention to the standards and, in turn, to my productions. I have to be very cognizant of what I am doing because the audios are being listened to by people of all ages, who have become very knowledgeable and savvy about media. The work you've done has created a new definition of the phrase *a collaborative effort.* I bet you didn't know that you, too, are part of the production process and that you've helped raise standards for all of us.[5]

In June 2008, Bruce Coville, author and founder of Full Cast Audio, spoke at the first Odyssey award ceremony about the background of the award. "We decided on the award's name because the Odyssey takes us right back to the Homeric roots of oral storytelling. The award symbol, the nautilus shell, ties us to Odysseus's voyage and the sea. The nautilus shell looks like the inner ear, recalling the sound waves that carry stories to us through audiobooks." Coville also addressed the significance of the award: "It is such a great thing to have this recognition, to have audiobooks placed at this level, saying, 'Yes, you are a full member of the children's literature community, of this library community.' It's an affirmation and validation of the work that's been done in the audiobook industry for over fifty years and the acceptance of spoken word literature in the educational world."[6]

AUDIOBOOK INDUSTRY AWARDS

The Audio Publishers Association (APA), formed in 1987, is the trade group that advocates for business interests of American audio publishers, narrators, and other allied entities. The group maintains an informative website, sponsors market research, compiles industry data, and hosts a yearly conference. Since 1996, the APA has celebrated the audio publishing field at the Audies Gala where the winners of the Audie Award are named, recognizing distinction in audiobook and spoken word entertainment. Lists of current and past Audie winners and finalists are available on the APA website (www.audiopub.org). Audiobook publishers may submit fee-based entries for consideration in the competition, which has over thirty categories for fiction, nonfiction, and foreign language productions. The Audies also recognize two premier categories, the Audiobook of the Year and Distinguished Achievement in Production, both of which may be children's or young adult titles. The criteria are different than the ALA awards, including items such as marketability, and the scope of titles considered is limited to those companies who choose to submit entries. The Audie judges—industry professionals and audiobook reviewers—select a broad array of excellent titles that are among the best of the industry for listeners of all ages.

Another recognizable industry award is the Grammy, awarded annually by the National Academy of Recording Arts and Sciences of the United States, a professional group that exists to honor achievements in the recording arts and support the music community. The Grammy is a peer-presented award that honors artistic achievement, technical proficiency, and overall excellence in the recording industry. From 1994 to 2011, the "Spoken Word Album for Children" Grammy was awarded, honoring recordings that are created and intended specifically for children with the focus of the album at least 51 percent newly recorded spoken word vs. music or song. From 1958 to 1994, spoken word recordings for children were eligible for the Grammy Award for Best Album for Children, then replaced by both the Best Spoken Word Album for Children and the Best Musical Album for Children Grammys. However, the category was eliminated as of 2012, reverting back to a single award for Best Children's Album, which includes albums containing at least 51 percent playing time of new musical or spoken word recordings that are created and intended specifically for children. Applicants for the Grammy, which may be submitted by recording companies or by academy members, are voted upon by all fee-paying Recording Academy members to be recognized as one of five nominees; a second ballot to all members determines the winner. The large number of voters from a broad spectrum of recording fields lends a unique aspect to the roster of Grammy winners. Past winners in both award categories may be found by searching the Grammy website database (www.grammy.com).

MEDIA RECOGNITION FOR AUDIOBOOKS

Audiobooks are regularly reviewed in both professional journals and consumer publications. Selectors reading reviews should target those that focus on facets of the audio production rather than an overview of the print book's content. *Booklist* magazine, published by the American Library Association, includes audiobook reviews geared toward public and school librarians with a special consideration for small and medium-sized libraries. The "Youth Audio" section focuses on titles for toddlers to teens, while "Adult Audio" notes titles with YA appeal. All materials reviewed in *Booklist* (and on Booklist Online, www.booklistonline.com) are recommended for purchase, with outstanding productions noted by a starred review. Feature columns in *Booklist* provide insight into audiobook production, listener's advisory, current trends, and listen-alike lists. Each January, *Booklist* names the previous year's best audiobooks for adults, children, and young adults in the Editors' Choice list, with one title selected as the Top of the List audiobook production. Each June, *Booklist* awards the annual Voice of Choice honor, recognizing a specific narrator's lasting impact in the world of audiobook narration. First awarded in 2008, the Voice of Choice highlights readers who have a substantial body of exemplary work in both adult and youth productions, providing a standard of excellence for audiobook narration.

AudioFile (www.audiofilemagazine.com), founded in 1992 by Robin Whitten, is a consumer magazine devoted to audiobooks, with a strong web presence. *AudioFile*'s feature articles give insights to audiobook enthusiasts, with topics ranging from the entertainment aspect of audiobooks to interviews with industry professionals. Each issue contains hundreds of reviews for both adults and youth with an Earphone Award icon noting titles that excel in narrative voice and style, vocal characterizations, appropriateness for the audio format, and enhancement of the text. *AudioFile* selects top titles in age and genre categories, publishing a yearly Best in Audiobooks list as well as the annual Golden Voice Award, recognizing narrators who have made significant contributions to the world of spoken-word recordings.

Publishers Weekly (www.publishersweekly.com) provides print and online industry news and reviews relating to audiobook publishing as well as a yearly Listen-Up Award list, which often contains children's and teen titles, published in January. *Library Journal*'s January Best Audiobooks list contains adult crossover titles of interest to teens, as well as classic titles with youth appeal. *School Library Journal* (www.schoollibraryjournal.com) and *The Horn Book* (www.hbook.com) include children and young adult audiobook reviews, as well as occasional features that address audiobook and transmedia publications. *Voice of Youth Advocates* (*VOYA*; www.voya .com) reviews audiobooks for young adults ages 12 to 18, and features a regular audiobook column. *Kirkus Reviews* (www.kirkusreviews.com) spearheaded the library community's first source for children's book app evaluation with the introduction of starred app reviews and offered a children's book app discovery engine geared toward consumers in 2011.

No matter the format, evaluation of spoken word literature requires recognition of the unique qualities of narration and sound production. Traditional audiobooks—as well as new varieties of transmedia that combine text, visual, and sound components—challenge selectors to assess both literary elements and multimedia design. Professional reviews offer guidance on the standards used to measure superior productions, while awards provide benchmarks of excellence. The subtle differences in criteria developed by library committees, industry awards, and professional reviewers allow a diverse selection of top-notch productions to be recognized each year, providing solid recommendations for purchase and listening pleasure.

SPOTLIGHT REFLECTION

The Power of Narration in the First Degree

BY JACK GANTOS

I MOST OFTEN WRITE books from the first-person point of view (the Jack Henry series, the Joey Pigza series, *Hole in My Life, The Love Curse of the Rumbaughs, Dead End in Norvelt)*, and it is my intent to befriend readers from the first sentence. The voice of the text grafts a bond with the reader. The tone, rhythm, word choice, sentence choreography all add up to the *voice* of the text, and it is this voice readers translate and hear amplified in their mind.

When I narrate a book, it's no surprise that the voice of the main character is the emotional rudder of the recording. Through the recorded voice, readers feel a deeper emotional intimacy with the character, the story— and with me, too. It is not that readers don't come to this emotional relationship through the act of reading, but the nuances revealed through a narration and the theatrical tones of the voice add dimension to a story. The dialogue and humor, the physical drama of the story, and the internal character responses project through the voice, providing a tangible sensory connection, salting the understanding of a story. Listeners savor fear and love, enthusiasm and gloom, self-loathing and self-admiration, goals met and missed, desires attained and desires spurned. The voice can create a great, dimensional portrait of the life of the book within the vast imagination of the reader.

For instance, after I wrote and recorded *Hole in My Life*, about my time in prison as a young man, I began to visit prisons—especially those for juvenile offenders that have an education program in the prison. The young men have to read the book before I arrive, but because of the rate of literacy in prisons, reading a book is an issue. The audiobook is used to make up for the disparity between readers and nonreaders. There have been times when I have entered a prison and heard the book being broadcast over the speaker system in the juvenile offender cell block. When I address the young men, they hear my voice—the same as the recorded voice—and we have an instant rapport. In no time we drift away from all the easy talk about drugs and money and girlfriends and get to the deeper points, the emotional points of shame and guilt and disappointment. I always feel that the audiobook allows listeners not only to see the story but to feel it in a way that leeches out their own feelings. As a result, we have great conversations.

I also recorded my Joey Pigza books, and when I speak to upper-elementary kids and middle schoolers, the children hear my voice and think I am Joey Pigza. Teachers use the audiobooks in classrooms all the time—a chapter a day. Kids often read along with the recording, which helps some with their reading skills. Even my recordings of the Rotten Ralph books are a silly hit among the primary kids. They laugh out loud at my voice because they recognize me as Ralph.

I could go on, but to boil this down, I think the recorded voice—my voice for my books—adds a note of authenticity and a very sincere emotional track to the book. When I listen to an audiobook, I can see the written words on the page. And when I read an evocative book, I can hear the full text in my mind. Writing and narrating go hand in glove. I admire them both. But the final confirmation of a perfect fit between written and spoken text is when a young person approaches me in a school and says, "You sound just like the character in my head." Now that is a voice I like to hear.

Jack Gantos is a Newbery, Printz, Sibert,
and National Book Award–honored author.

NOTES

1. "Notable Children's Recordings," Association for Library Service to Children (ALSC), ALA, http://www.ala.org/alsc/awardsgrants/notalists/ncr.

2. "Amazing Audiobooks for Young Adults," Young Adult Library Services Association, ALA, www.ala.org/yalsa/audiobooks.

3. Ibid.

4. "Welcome to the Odyssey Award Home Page!" ALSC, ALA, 2011, www.ala.org/ala/mgrps/divs/alsc/awardsgrants/bookmedia/odysseyaward/index.cfm.

5. Mary Burkey, "The Booklist Odyssey Interview: Arnie Cardillo," *Booklist* (March 1, 2008): 79.

6. Bruce Coville, "Remarks during the Odyssey Awards Presentation" (unpublished speech, June 6, 2008). From a recording made by the author.

8 Into the Future, Listening to the Past

AS THE PRINT PUBLISHING world is transformed by e-books, the audiobook community responds with "Been there, done that," reflecting the many seismic shifts in production and distribution technology, from LPs to streaming media. Back in the twentieth century, Audible founded the first online audiobook store in 1995, selling a new-fangled device—the MP3 player—that could play audiobook digital files in a copy-protected proprietary format.[1] Amazon did much the same when popularizing the e-book through the introduction of the Kindle e-Reader with a laser-sharp focus on building a consumer base. Travel back in time to the year 2000, the launch of OverDrive Media Content Reserve and the birth of library-friendly audiobook downloads.[2] These early digital audiobook service providers paved the way for e-book download content models for consumers and library patrons. But will audiobooks survive in the ever-evolving app-driven, enhanced-media digital marketplace?

FORMATS AND THE FUTURE: CHANGE HAPPENS

Audiobook fans have said their sad good-byes to both vinyl records and the cassette tape, the latter of which so revolutionized the marketplace in the 1970s that audiobook old-timers still refer to downloads as "books on tape." If the near-death of the cassette is the audiobook equivalent of the hardcover on life-support, the book publishing world can breathe a sigh of relief: history shows that the increase in audiobook downloads has consistently equaled or exceeded the lost percentage of physical-format market, according to the Audio Publishers Association.[3] Plus, the digital format has converted never-before listeners into audiobook aficionados—just as e-book readers are increasing the amount of books read. These newly converted listeners attuned to a professional narrator's nuanced and expressive reading are loathe to substitute the synthetic text-to-speech function on their e-reader, preferring instead the human warmth of a storyteller's voice heard via audiobooks.

Books are morphing into digital data on a variety of players that have the ability to provide both sound and video. Savvy digital readers are accustomed to instant access to content and seamless syncing between devices. As these words are being written, who are the top consumers of apps that merge text and voice? Techie toddlers wielding their parents' smartphones and tablet computers lead the way, with publishers such as Oceanhouse Media and Disney Digital Books syncing text and audio along with full-color illustrations from the books. Streaming audio plus video for preschool to middle grades is available from Tales2Go, an app-based subscription service, which offers licensed content from publishers such as Recorded Books and Scholastic in a format friendly to both consumers and schools.[4] Many public and school libraries provide TumbleBooks for patrons, a digital service that combines animation, sound, music and narration with existing books for toddlers to teens, offering synced content that may be streamed or downloaded.[5] Major publishers such as Macmillan are introducing interactive first-word picture-book apps, bringing an enhanced board-book experience to even the youngest reader.[6]

A growing number of long-established audiobook publishers have app-based audiobooks available for adults, syncing text and professional audiobook narration with added content. Moving Tales creates what they term a "state-of-the-art digital 'mash-up' of methods from the worlds of ebook publishing, graphic novels, film and interactive media."[7] Moving Tales titles such as *The Pedlar Lady of Gushing Cross* transform the time-honored readalong format into a multimedia experience for adults, prompting the reviewer Richard MacManus to ask, "Is this the future of eBooks?"[8] Every librarian echoes Marshall Breeding's concern: "How do we make our technology investments not only future-proof but also more able to endure the cycles of change that will continuously transform libraries?"[9]

DOCUMENTING THE DIGITAL SHIFT

Let's take a look at statistics that document the growth of digital audiobooks in the twenty-first century. A 2009 study by Barbara A Genco and Michael Santangelo focused on e-book adoption in forty-one larger U.S. public libraries; valuable information about digital audiobooks was also documented. When asked "What year did your library begin your eBooks/Downloadable content collection?" the respondents noted:

1997–1999 (4.9%)
2000–2002 (31.7%)
2003–2005 (14.6%)
2006–2008 (46.3%)
2009 (2.4%)

Only one library did not offer digital content at the time of the survey. Of the responding libraries, 87.8 percent offered e-audiobooks by 2009. Thirty-three libraries responded to the question "Approximately how many downloadable items (all formats) does your library hold?" with an average number of 13,288 units. When asked "Do you reallocate funds from your physical materials formats to buy electronic, downloadable copies? Is your library buying fewer 'physical' Audiobooks and instead purchasing more electronic copies of eAudiobooks?" 46.3 percent responded yes, 36.6 percent responded no, and 19.5 percent were considering doing so.

Genco and Santangelo's survey illustrates that the first decade of the twenty-first century was a time of radical change in library collection development and delivery, sparking a switch from physical to digital materials and budget dollars. The survey documented the growth of digital downloads in the three years prior to the study—from spectacular growth at Hennepin County Public Library (1200%), to high growth (100–300%) reported by ten libraries, to average growth (31–99%) reported by eight libraries, and to low growth (5.4% and 30%) reported by seven libraries. Genco noted that, according to the results, "the first foray of many American public libraries into the eBook format began with the launch of netLibrary in 1998. Interestingly though, over the last five years most American public libraries . . . have begun to work with a single Cleveland (Ohio) based company—OverDrive. In less than five years OverDrive has partnered with publishers and with 8500 public libraries in the US and Canada to license and deliver over 100,000 titles to public and school library users."[10]

According to David Burleigh, director of marketing for OverDrive Media, total audiobook circulation through that company in U.S. public libraries in 2009 was 6,947,027, with 791,095 children's and YA titles (as designated by publisher age category) circulated, or approximately 11 percent of total circulation. In 2010, the number increased to about 12 percent, with 1,270,572 youth titles downloaded within a total circulation of 10,615,325 audiobooks accessed through OverDrive. In the first six months of 2011, children's and YA circulation increased to 13 percent of total circulation, with 1,019,626 youth titles downloaded within a total circulation of 7,781,753 digital audiobooks. Although this slow but steady growth of library audiobook downloads by young digital natives shows that listenership has increased, libraries can clearly increase the proportion of youth audio downloads through focused initiatives, such as including youth services librarians in audiobook consortium purchase decisions and removing format restraints from budgetary items, allowing youth book funds to be used to buy literature in any format.[11]

GIVE 'EM WHAT THEY WANT

According to a 2010 survey from the Audio Publishers Association of both audiobook publishers and consumers, adult audiobook listeners are better educated and have higher incomes than nonlisteners, are more likely to own an MP3 player and e-book reader, and are also avid print readers. Seventy-four percent of frequent adult listeners report their children also listen to audiobooks, yet 59 percent of all adult listeners reported that they would prefer their child read books rather than listen. This finding highlights the need for parent education of the literacy benefits of audiobooks found in chapter 2. However, the influence of parents in fostering youth appreciation of audiobooks is apparent, as most listeners were introduced to audios as entertainment during a long car trip, and enjoying audiobooks together as a family was a common survey reply. Adult respondents also expressed the opinion that audiobooks expose children to books they might not otherwise read and increase children's love of reading. These survey results offer support for libraries who want to initiate parent-child audiobook discussion groups, create family vacation listening promotions, or pilot school-library collaboration to publicize audiobooks as a way to foster a love of literature.

The 2010 APA consumer study found that of the general population of teens ages 15 to 17, 36 percent of respondents were audiobook listeners. These teen listeners were avid consumers of print literature as well, with 59 percent reading a book in the past week—a fact that serves to dispel the mistaken notion that only struggling readers listen to audiobooks. The most common reasons teen listeners started listening to audiobooks were for entertainment on a long trip (46%), because parents or siblings listened (30%), or because of a teacher or class assignment (29%). Fourteen percent noted that they had downloaded an audiobook from the library, selecting formats based on whether they can play the title in their car or computer. Teen listeners choose audiobooks based on the title's subject matter, preferring best sellers and general fiction, with the top two genres comedy (30%) and mystery/thriller/suspense (25%). Selectors should note that some adult consumers responded that they obtained youth audiobooks through homeschool connections, their church, or a Christian bookstore, highlighting the need for religious and Christian fiction genre titles in the collection and targeted outreach to these audiobook patrons. In the 2008 APA consumer study, when asked where they searched for audiobooks, teen listeners were most likely to turn first to the library (44%) and then retail sellers (25%), with recommendations from friends (29%), websites (28%), teachers (27%), and librarians (26%). Busy teens appreciate audiobooks while commuting or as a way to multitask, but more than half of all teens responded in 2010 that they listen while relaxing at home—three key, but distinct, characteristics that, along with all the survey data, can guide library audiobook purchases, promotions and displays.[12]

An initiative to acquaint more teens with digital audiobooks was launched in 2010, as major publishers provided free downloads through Sync (www.audiobooksync.com), pairing popular YA titles, often the first in a series, with classic literature commonly found on high school reading lists—for example, *The Hunger Games* by Suzanne Collins (Scholastic 2008) with Shirley Jackson's *The Lottery* (Audio Partners 1998). Coordinated through the Audiobook Community social network (www.facebook.com/

audiobookcommunity), Sync's success shows the power of providing tools to educate users and promoting youth audiobooks through social media. In 2010, Sync's inaugural year, there were 17,485 downloads of eighteen free titles supplied by eleven audiobook publishers, over just nine weeks, to 506 individual Sync group members and through 272 library or school-based summer programs. In 2011, the number of downloads rose to 20,768 titles in the same time period—an increase of nearly 19 percent. This unique initiative that actively partners with school and public libraries has proven to be very successful, with 69.6 percent of surveyed Sync first-time audiobook listeners stating they will continue to listen to audiobooks in the future.[13]

READING THE CRYSTAL BALL

The rapid pace of change in the publishing world shows no signs of slowing down, resulting in libraries learning to adapt in order to provide the best for patrons. Varying formats and instant accessibility will expand the role of multimedia literature, leading to streaming digital content everywhere. This explosion of options opens the world of literary excellence to young library patrons, many who previously would never have checked out a physical book. Michele Cobb, an executive at AudioGO, reflects on the future:

> With the changes in technology the audiobook industry will continue to grow, more titles will be published and the introduction of the format to more people will grow not just in the US, but across the globe. Libraries will be a part of this explosion, as new models of digital audiobook lending allow patrons wider access, but still provide reasonable royalty returns for authors and rights-holders. Audiobook formats will also continue to evolve with new technology. We know most audiobook listeners are also book readers, and new, seamlessly integrated hybrids of audiobooks and e-books will allow listeners to alternate their input—swapping eye-reading to ear-listening on the same book with just one click.[14]

Children and teens live in a world where literature is being transformed into new and engaging formats. As the very definitions of *reading* and *book* are rewritten, new digital formats allow a reinterpretation of literacy. The ability to shift seamlessly from image to text to sound will be part of every young person's transliterate education. Yet no matter how much the medium of the message may change, a core truth remains: to be human is to share our stories. The aural appreciation of story is the oldest form of literature, and voice captured on audiobook communicates an author's words in a way that re-creates the oral tradition. As libraries are reinvented in the digital age, Ranganathan's Laws of Library Science—"Every reader his or her book" and "Every book its reader"[15]—are revised as "Every patron his or her story" and "Every story its format," allowing literature to find new appreciation from new audiences.

From the first Bubble Book in 1917 to the appearance of Dr. Seuss apps nearly a century later, the human voice has been a constant in each new multimedia format. Ranganathan considered the library a growing organism—and the evolution of audiobooks in libraries, from shellac 78 rpm records to digital downloads, while retaining the integral element of voice as part of the organic whole, demonstrates this principle. Recorded voice connects us to literature in its original form; innovative technology creates a virtual storyteller's circle for young listeners. The twenty-first-century library is the transfer point for passing the spark of great stories to children, lighting a fire with new formats that speak the timeless language of literature.

NOTES

1. "Audible Milestones," Audible.com, accessed May 24, 2012, http://about.audible.com/audible-milestones/.

2. "OverDrive Media: About," accessed May 24, 2012, www.overdrive.com/About

3. "Audiobook Sales Increase in 2009," Audio Publishers Association, www.audiopub.org/PDFs/SalesSurveyPR62810.pdf.

4. "About Us," Tales2Go, accessed May 24, 2012, http://www.tales2go.com/about-audiobook-app.

5. "About the TumbleBook Library," TumbleBooks Library, accessed May 24, 2012,www.tumblebooks.com/library/asp/about_tumblebooks.asp.

6. Esther Bochner, "Macmillan Publishers Launches Two New Apps for Young Children," e-mail message to author, December 2010.

7. "Moving Tales: About," accessed May 24, 2012, http://moving-tales .com/about.html.

8. Richard MacManus, "Moving Tales: Do Animated E-books Have a Future?" New York Times, September 1, 2010, www.nytimes.com/ external/readwriteweb/2010/09/01/01readwriteweb-moving-tales -do-animated-ebooks-have-a-futu-49448.html.

9. Marshall Breeding, "Can We Future-Proof Library Automation?" Computers in Libraries 30, no. 2 (March 1, 2010): 29–31.

10. Barbara A. Genco, "It's Been Geometric! Documenting the Growth and Acceptance of E-books in America's Urban Public Libraries," July 24, 2009, www.ifla.org/files/hq/papers/ifla75/212-genco-en.pdf.

11. David Burleigh, in discussion with the author, July 8, 2010.

12. Member Resources, Audio Publishers Association, 2010, www.audiopub.org/members-archive.asp.

13. Kirsten Cappy, in discussion with the author, Sept 6, 2011.

14. Michele Cobb, in discussion with the author, July 19, 2011.

15. Ranganathan, S. R., The Five Laws of Library Science. (London: G. Blunt and Sons, 1957).

AUDIOBOOK LEXICON

ABRIDGED. Original work edited by a professional abridger, with the goal of staying true to the spirit and content of a book.

ACCENT. Of a specific nationality or region, e.g., German or midwestern, or a socioeconomic class.

ACTUALITY AUDIO. Section of audio from another source (e.g., interviews, animal sounds) added to the original studio recording.

AMBIENCE. Sound quality that comes from the recording studio environment rather than directly from the sound source.

ATTRIBUTIVES. Identifying phrases such as "he said" and "she whispered."

AUDIO CUE MISMATCH. Audio mismatch with the source visual or text; a sound effect or added music that does not match the text, or in readalongs, match the illustration.

Compiled and edited by Mary Burkey, July 2011. Originally printed in *AudioFile* October/November 2007 as "Talking the Talk," by Mary Burkey. The audio producers below generously contributed to the creation of the above list: Arnie Cardillo (Live Oak Media), Michele Cobb (AudioGo), Bruce Coville (Full Cast Audio), Tim Ditlow (Brilliance Audio), Todd and Brett Hobin (Hobin Studios), Paul Gagne (Weston Woods), Eileen Hutton (Brilliance Audio), Troy Juliar (Recorded Books), Pete Pantelis, David Rapkin (David Rapkin Audio Production).

AUDIOBOOK ORIGINAL. An audiobook with no print or e-book counterpart, or a title that is available in audio prior to print or e-book publication.

BONUS MATERIAL. Extras added to an audiobook or items from the print title that may be on audio, such as a time line, a glossary, or an author interview.

BOOK APP. An interactive digital book that is accessed on a device such as a tablet computer or mobile phone and may include synchronized text, animations, audio, and more.

BREAK POINT. A logical and appropriate stopping point of audio medium segments or other break in the audio production.

BREATHY. A quality of mouth sound; sharp or odd breaths by a narrator; an audible breath at a sentence break.

BRIGHT. A sound quality that is clear and sharp.

CADENCE. Rhythm of speech, created through modulation and inflection.

CHOPPY EDIT. A noticeable or abrupt editing of sound.

CLAM SHELL. A hard case designed for multiple circulations and used for library and school editions of physical audiobooks.

CLARITY OF NARRATION. Clear and understandable reading; diction.

CLARITY OF PRODUCTION. Recording clarity; clean sound throughout a recording, not muddy or muted.

CLIPPED EDIT. The end of a word cut off in audio editing.

CONSISTENCY. A narrator maintaining energy and character voicings throughout a recording, even if narration was recorded at different times.

CONTEXT OF LINE. Maintaining meaning of text through expression and emphasis.

CONTINUOUS RECORD. A narration recorded in extended segments without interruption, as opposed to *punch-in* edits.

COVER ART. The art on an audiobook's packaging. The audiobook may match the hardcover or paperback print item's cover art, or may be entirely different.

CULTURAL AUTHENTICITY. Matching the reader and the culture of a character so that accents or dialects are authentic, not stereotyped. May also include authentic music.

DIALECT. Of a specific group of people; e.g., Appalachian.

DIGITAL DISTORTION. A cracking or blurry sound when volume exceeds the upper digital range.

DIGITAL DOWNLOAD. An audiobook available as a digital file, accessed and downloaded directly to a computer or playback device, needing no delivery medium.

DIGITAL-ONLY. An audiobook distributed by a publisher solely as a download.

DIRECT-TO-CONSUMER DIGITAL. A digital audiobook that needs no distribution media (such as MP3, CD, preloaded digital player) and is accessed by a playback device.

DIRECTOR. A person hired to direct the talent in the studio during an audiobook recording.

DISTRIBUTION MEDIA. A method of delivering audio (MP3, CD) that requires another playback device, such as a CD player.

DOWNLOAD SERVICE VENDOR. An arrangement of an individual or library system to purchase licensed audiobooks from an Internet retailer; e.g., Audible, OverDrive.

DRAMATIC DYNAMIC RANGE. A controlled range of volume, with emotion shown through energy and not resulting in uneven sound levels.

DRAMATIZATION. An adaptation, usually multivoiced, often with sound effects, music, and interaction; often called *audio drama* or *radio theater.* Not synonymous with *multivoiced.*

DRM. Abbreviation for *digital rights management,* technologies used by publishers or distributors that control access or usage of digital audio.

DRY MOUTH. A clicking mouth sound.

EMOTION. The degree to which the emotional content of text is expressed, explicating the meaning of text through the voice.

ENERGY. A quality of the narrator's reading that engenders listener engagement.

ENHANCED PRODUCT. Material added to an audiobook package, such as illustrations, games, computer files, or video; see also *value-added*.

EQUALIZATION. A pleasant and nonfatiguing tonal quality over the full range of audio spectrum of the audio format.

EXECUTIVE PRODUCER. A person employed by an audio publisher who oversees the total audiobook production and funding.

EXPRESSION. The overall performance quality; the range a narrator uses that engenders listener engagement.

EXTRAS. Forewords, afterwords, glossaries, dedications, photo captions or notes, and miscellaneous words that appear in picture book illustrations.

FADE IN, FADE OUT. Bringing music or a sound effect in or out of the recording, gradually or steeply; also known as *ramping* a sound in or out.

FLAT. Narration that seems dull, unemotional, monotone.

FORMATTING. Editing a recording to fit on cassette (104 minutes), CD (80 minutes), or MP3 (12-plus hours).

FULL-CAST NARRATION. Multiple narrators performing as individual characters during an ensemble reading.

FULLY VOICED. A single narrator using a range of multiple character differentiations and voicings in a solo performance.

GLUEY. A sticky mouth sound.

HARDWARE. The physical device that is used to access an audio medium.

HISS. Audible background noise; unwarranted high-frequency noise.

HOLLOW. A sound quality that echoes or lacks depth.

HOT. An audio quality that is too loud or intense.

ID3 TAGS. Metadata that allows a CD or digital audio player to display the track and title information.

INCIDENTAL MUSIC. Music at the beginning, end, or other point in a production.

INDEX POINTS/TRACK POINTS. Invisible markings that allow the listener to jump to points on audio file. May vary in length, depending on producer.

INFLECTION. Overall performance quality, rise, and fall of the voice pitch used for expression.

INTRO. The part of a recording where the title, author, and narrator are identified.

JUICY. A wet mouth sound; saliva noise.

LICENSED AUDIOBOOK. Audiobook available for legal purchase through authorized distributor by arrangement with the producer.

LIFELESS. Sound quality that does not engage the listener, dry.

LINER NOTES. Text or visual material describing the production. May be printed on a sleeve or wrap, or available digitally.

LIP SMACKS. A type of mouth sound.

LISTENER ENGAGEMENT. The involvement of the listener in the production.

MEDIUM. A means that provides transmission or storage of information.

MISSING TEXT. An error where text from the source is missing in the finished audio production.

MIX. Combining distinct tracks or audio segments into a unified production.

MOOD. The emotional ambience of the audio, created by the narrator's voice, music, and sound effects.

MOUTH CLICK. A type of mouth sound.

MP3. An audio encoding format that compresses data, used for downloaded audiobooks and for MP3s that hold more than eighty minutes.

MUDDY. A sound quality where the audio is muffled or indistinct, usually due to an excess of bass energy or missing mid to high frequencies.

MULTIVOICED PRODUCTION. An audiobook with more than one narrator, but not necessarily an actor for each character, nor recorded as an ensemble at the same time.

MUSHY. A vocal quality with a lack of precision in diction.

MUSIC CUE/TAG. Music used to note a scene change, identify a character, depict a mood, reference a time period, or accent some other aspect of production.

MUSIC LIBRARY. Stock music licensed from a vendor, used in the audiobook production.

MUSICAL BED. Music heard under the narration throughout portions or large parts of the audiobook.

MUSICAL INTRO. The music at beginning of a production.

MUSICAL OUTRO. The music at end of a production.

NARRATOR. A person who delivers the content of the audiobook.

NARRATOR MATCH. The casting of a narrator who suits the character's age and gender as well as the book's time period, setting, and mood.

NOISE-GATING. An abrupt edit resulting in clipped words or silence between words.

OFF-MIC. Sound when the narrator is recorded away from the microphone or the narrator's mouth turns away from the microphone.

ORIGINAL MUSIC. A musical score that is composed expressly for the audiobook production.

OUT-OF-SYNC. Mismatched sound and visual of an audiobook, when the narrator's voice doesn't track with the text in a production such as a readalong picture book.

OUTRO. Information at end of a production. May contain the program title, the narrator, the author, publisher information, and copyright notice.

PACING OF NARRATION. The rate at which the narrator reads; may be too fast or too slow.

PACING OF PRODUCTION. A passage paced correctly for the dramatic arc of a story.

PAGE RATE. How long it takes a narrator to complete a page of text. Also known as *pickup* and *reader acquisition rate*.

PAGE TURN/PAPER NOISE. Studio noise.

PARTIALLY VOICED. A single narrator primarily using a *straight read* with a few major character differentiations.

PEAKY. A sound quality that is too high in volume or energy level.

PITCH RANGE. A high or low range of sound.

PLAYBACK DEVICE. Hardware, such as an iPod, a cell phone, or a CD player, that allows the playback of distribution media (cassette tape, CD) or digital files (MP3, WMA).

PLOSIVE OR WIND POP. A noticeable microphone noise or mouth pop sound, typically formed by *pp*, *tt*, and *ff* sounds.

PODIOBOOK. A serialized, unpublished book available via the Internet directly from the author as an audio podcast, usually for free.

PRELOADED AUDIO PLAYBACK DEVICE. A hardware device that is preloaded with a digital audiobook; self-contained, e.g., a Playaway.

PRESENCE. A sound quality that feels authentic or actual, as if the listener is present in the action of the story.

PRODUCER. A person hired by the executive producer who hires talent, books studio time, and handles financial details.

PROSODY. Vocal melody and tonal inflection.

PUBLIC DOMAIN. Content not restricted by copyright. Such audiobooks may be recorded by volunteers and distributed through Librivox or an audiobook publisher.

PUNCH-IN, PUNCH AND ROLL. Narration edited as it is recorded, requiring a stop-and-start interruption to the reading, as opposed to a *continuous record*.

READALONG. An audiobook meant to be listened to while following along with a picture book's text and illustrations.

READER ENGAGEMENT. The perception that the narrator is actively involved in the production.

REPEATED SENTENCE/WORD. A production error where poor editing results in repeated content.

RICH. Recording clarity; clean sound throughout an audiobook, not muddy or muted.

SEQUENCE ANNOUNCEMENT. A vocal prompt at the end of a CD, cassette, or audio portion; also known as a *tag line*.

SIBILANT. The distortion or overload of sound resulting in an over-emphasis of *sss, fff,* and *ch* sounds.

SILENT INTERVAL. Silence, such as the space between chapters.

SIMULTANEOUS RELEASE. A release date of an audiobook at the same time as the print book release.

SLEEVE. The packaging material that holds printed information or CDs.

SOUND EFFECT. A sound used to establish action, time, place, or mood; an added audio effect that is referenced in the text or illustrations, often found in readalongs.

SOUND LEVEL. The overall volume of a recording—ideally consistent, not variable or uneven.

SOUNDSCAPE. The total sound environment; the created audible world of the audiobook.

SPECIAL OR BONUS FEATURE. Any author interview or other audio material not found in the original text; also known as *value added*.

SPOKEN WORD PERFORMANCE. An audio presentation that is a recording of a seminar, lecture, or comedy routine, for example.

STRAIGHT READ. A narrator reading in his or her natural voice.

STREAMING AUDIO. A digital audiobook playback over a live Internet connection.

STRESS. A narrator's emphasizing a word or syllable. *Stress* on a particular syllable or word results in changed meaning.

STUDIO NOISE. The noise made by clothing, jewelry, page turns, body movements, and other extraneous sound that is captured in the recording.

TAG LINE. A comment at the beginning or end of an audio segment, such as "End of side two. Please insert . . ."

TAIL. The end of a production.

TALENT. A person hired to read; may be an actor, author, professional narrator, or celebrity.

TALKING BOOK PROGRAM. The audiobook service provided by the National Library Services to the Blind and Physically Handicapped.

TEXT-TO-SPEECH SOFTWARE. A computer program that allows software to create an artificial voice that translates text directly into a digital file.

THIN. A sound quality that strains the ear or is difficult to hear.

THROAT SWALLOW. A body noise.

TINNY. A sound quality that is artificial or electronic, or lacks low frequency.

TOC FILE. Abbreviation for *table of contents* file—metadata that ensures that sound files play the audiobook in correct sequence.

TOP. The beginning of an audiobook.

TRACK POINT/INDEX POINT. An invisible marking that allows the listener to jump to a point on an audio file; may vary in length, depending on the producer.

TUMMY RUMBLE. A body noise.

UNABRIDGED. A complete, unaltered work.

UNDERSCORE. The music under a narration.

UNVOICED. A single narrator performing a *straight read* in his or her natural voice with no characterization.

UPCUT. A choppy, noticeable, or abrupt editing of sound at the beginning of a word.

VALUE-ADDED. Extras added to audio title, such as visual content or an author interview.

VOCABLE. A nonword sound that evokes meaning, such as a click, grunt, or sigh.

VOICE ACTOR. A professional narrator.

WALL OF PERFORMANCE. A barrier that may be apparent to a listener who is aware of the voice actor's performance, or one that may be removed by a skilled narrator.

WIDOWS AND ORPHANS. A sentence (*widow*) or text fragment (*orphan*) split by an audio production side, CD, or segment change.

WOOFING THE MICROPHONE. Narrating that causes pops or plosives.

WORD COUNT. Used to estimate recording length. The typical narrator reads approximately 154 words per minute, or 9,200 words per hour.

WRAP. The paper with production information that slips in the outer packaging of an audiobook.

RECOMMENDED READING

BEAVIN, KRISTI. "Audiobooks: Four Styles of Narration." *Horn Book Magazine* 72, no. 5 (September 1996): 566–573.

BEDNAR, LUCY. "Audiobooks and the Reassertion of Orality: Walter J. Ong and Others Revisited."*CEA Critic* 73, no. 1 (Fall 2010): 74–85.

BEERS, KYLENE. "Listen While You Read." *School Library Journal* 44, no. 5 (April 1998): 30–36.

BERNINGER, VIRGINIA W., AND ROBERT D. ABBOTT. "Listening Comprehension, Oral Expression, Reading Comprehension, and Written Expression: Related Yet Unique Language Systems in Grades 1, 3, 5, and 7." *Journal of Educational Psychology* 102, no. 3 (August 2010): 635–651.

BIRD, ELIZABETH. "Planet APP." *School Library Journal* 57, no. 1 (January 2011): 26–31.

BOMER, RANDY. "Reading with the Mind's Ear: Listening to Text as a Mental Action." *Journal of Adolescent & Adult Literacy* 49, no. 6 (March 1, 2006): 524–535.

BOOKS ON TAPE. "Audiobooks and Literacy Toolbox." Books on Tape. Accessed July 9, 2011. http://library.booksontape.com/audiobooks andliteracy.cfm.

BURKEY, MARY. "The Audible Art of Poetry." *Book Links* 17, no. 5 (May 2008): 34–35.

———. "Encouraging Family Listening." *Book Links* 17, no. 6 (July 2008): 26.

———. "Long-Form Listening." *Book Links* 18, no. 6 (July 2009): 26–27.

———. "Audiobooks Alive with the Sound of Music." *Book Links* 18, no. 1 (September 2008): 24–25.

———. "The *Booklist* Odyssey Interview: Dan Musselman." *Booklist* 107, no. 12 (February 15, 2011): 82.

CAMPBELL, ROBYN. "The Power of the Listening Ear." *English Journal* 100, no. 5 (May 1, 2011): 66–70.

CLARK, RUTH COX. "Audiobooks for Children: Is This Really Reading?" *Children & Libraries: The Journal of the Association for Library Service to Children* 5, no. 1 (Spring 2007): 49–50.

COLLET, LIONEL, ET AL. "Auditory Processing Disorder in Children with Reading Disabilities: Effect of Audiovisual Training." *Brain* 130, no. 11 (November 1, 2007): 2915–2928.

CYLKE, FRANK KURT, MICHAEL M. MOODIE, AND ROBERT E. FISTICK. "Serving the Blind and Physically Handicapped in the United States of America." *Library Trends* 55, no. 4 (Spring 2007): 796–808.

DESSOFF, ALAN. "Resources to Support Disabled Learners." *District Administration* 44, no. 6 (May 2008): 49–52.

DOCTOROW, CORY. "Can You Hear Me Now?" *Publishers Weekly* 256, no. 49 (December 7, 2009): 31.

DONOHUE, NANETTE. "Nurturing Your Media." *Library Journal* 133, no. 19 (November 15, 2008): 32–35.

ERDMAN, JACQUELYN MARIE, AND BOHYUN KIM. "What Is Your Library Doing about Emerging Technologies? A Report of the LITA Emerging Technologies Interest Group Program, American Library Association Annual Meeting, Washington, DC, June, 2010." *Technical Services Quarterly* 28, no. 3 (July 2011): 339–346.

FARRELL, BETH. "The Lowdown on Audio Downloads." *Library Journal* 135, no. 9 (May 15, 2010): 26–29.

FRUM, DAVID. "Reading by Ear." *Commentary* 127, no. 5 (May 2009): 94–96.

FUES, MARIANNE COLE. "Getting Teens to Read with Their Ears." *Library Media Connection* 27, no. 6 (May 1, 2009): 54.

GOLDSMITH, FRANCISCA. "Earphone English." *School Library Journal* 48, no. 5 (May 2002): 50–53.

GREEN, JOHN. "The Future of Reading: Don't Worry. It Might Be Better Than You Think." *School Library Journal* 56, no. 1 (January 1, 2010): 24–28.

GROVER, SHARON, AND LIZETTE HANNEGAN. "Hear and Now: Connecting Outstanding Audiobooks to Library and Classroom Instruction." *Teacher Librarian* 35, no. 3 (February 2008): 17–21.

———. "Not Just for Listening." *Book Links* 14, no. 5 (May 2005): 16–19.

HARMON, AMY. "Loud, Proud, Unabridged: It Is Too Reading!" *New York Times,* (May 26, 2005): 1.

HOLLEY, PAM SPENCER. "The *Booklist* Odyssey Interview: Troy Juliar." *Booklist* 105, no. 14 (March 15, 2009): 72.

HOY, SUSAN. "What Talking Books Have to Say: Issues and Options for Public Libraries." *Australasian Public Libraries and Information Services* 22, no. 4 (December 2009): 164–180.

IRWIN, WILLIAM. "Reading Audio Books." *Philosophy & Literature* 33, no. 2 (October 2009): 358–368.

JEMTEGAARD, KRISTI. "Readers vs. Listeners." *Booklist* 101, no. 15 (April 2005): 139.

———. "Audio Poetry: A Call to Words." *Horn Book Magazine* 81, no. 3 (May 2005): 357–364.

KAYE, ALAN L. "Audio 2008: Audio Fixation." *Library Journal* 133, no. 9 (May 15, 2008): 34–37.

KOZLOFF, SARAH. "Audio Books in Visual Culture." *Journal of American Culture* 18, no. 4 (Winter 1995): 83–96.

KUZYK, RAYA. "Audio Paradiso." *Library Journal* 136, no. 7 (April 15, 2011): 20–30.

LEARNING ALLY. "Learning through Listening: Classroom Tools, Sound Advice." Learning through Listening. Last modified 2011. www.learningthroughlistening.org.

LIBRIVOX. "LibriVox: Free Audiobooks." Accessed July 19, 2011. LibriVox. http://librivox.org.

MARTIN, ALBERT T. "The Oral Interpreter and the Phonograph." *Quarterly Journal of Speech* 38, no. 2 (April 1952): 195–198.

MAUGHAN, SHANNON. "Audiobooks 2.0." *Publishers Weekly* 257, no. 19 (May 10, 2010): 11–16.

MEDIATORE, KAITE, AND MARY K. CHELTON. "Reading with Your Ears." *Reference & User Services Quarterly* 42, no. 4 (Summer 2003): 318–324.

MILANI, ANNA, MARIA LUISA LORUSSO, AND MASSIMO MOLTENI. "The Effects of Audiobooks on the Psychosocial Adjustment of Pre-adolescents and Adolescents with Dyslexia." *Dyslexia* 16, no. 1 (February 2010): 87–97.

MYRICK, ELLEN. "Say It with Music: Audiobooks with Pizzazz." *Booklist* 105, no. 5 (November 2008): 64.

RECORDED BOOKS. "Teacher Resource List." Recorded Books. Accessed July 24, 2011. www.recordedbooks.com/index.cfm?fuseaction=school .resource_list.

RICH, MOTOKO. "Literacy Debate: Online, R U Really Reading?" *New York Times,* July 27, 2008., 1.

SARICKS, JOYCE. "LA: Essentials of Listening Advisory." *Booklist* 104, no. 21 (July 2008): 16.

———. "At Leisure: Rediscovering the Classics—through Audiobooks." *Booklist* 106, no. 19/20 (June 2010): 29.

SKOUGE, JAMES, KAVITA RAO, AND PRECILLE BOISVERT. "Promoting Early Literacy for Diverse Learners Using Audio and Video Technology." *Early Childhood Education Journal* 35, no. 1 (August 2007): 5–11.

STERN, CATHERINE. "The Role of Audiobooks in Academic Libraries." *College & Undergraduate Libraries* 18, no. 1 (January 2011): 77–91.

THOMPSON, RICHARD A. "Developing Listening Skills to Improve Reading." *Education* 91, no. 3 (February 1971): 261–266.

VARDELL, SYLVIA. "My Odyssey Voyage." *Booklist* 104, no. 19/20 (June 2008): 124.

WELLS, HENRY W. "Literature and the Phonograph." *Quarterly Journal of Speech* 29, no. 1 (February 1943): 68–73.

WYSOCKI, BARBARA. "Louder, Please: For Some Kids, the Best Way to Read Is to Turn Up the Volume." *School Library Journal* 51, no. 4 (April 1, 2005): S10.

INDEX

You may also be interested in

Read to Succeed: Strategies to Engage Children and Young People in Reading for Pleasure

EDITED BY JOY COURT

This much-needed collection covers all aspects of promoting reading to and with young people, along with models of current practices and inspiration for future developments.

ISBN: 978-1-8560-4747-0
288 pages / 6" x 9"

LISTENING TO LEARN: AUDIOBOOKS SUPPORTING LITERACY
SHARON GROVER AND LIZETTE D. HANNEGAN
ISBN: 978-0-8389-1107-5

TECHNOLOGY AND LITERACY: 21ST CENTURY LIBRARY PROGRAMMING FOR CHILDREN AND TEENS
JENNIFER NELSON AND KEITH BRAAFLADT
ISBN: 978-0-8389-1108-2

YOUNG ADULT LITERATURE: FROM ROMANCE TO REALISM
MICHAEL CART
ISBN: 978-0-8389-1045-0

THE READERS' ADVISORY GUIDE TO GRAPHIC NOVELS
FRANCISCA GOLDSMITH
ISBN: 978-0-8389-1008-5

BOOKLIST'S 1000 BEST YOUNG ADULT BOOKS, 2000–2010
EDITORS OF BOOKLIST
ISBN: 978-0-8389-1150-1

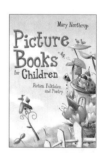

PICTURE BOOKS FOR CHILDREN: FICTION, FOLKTALES, AND POETRY
MARY NORTHRUP
ISBN: 978-0-8389-1144-0